Keys to Math Success Grades K-1

"Fun" Standard-Based Activities to Boost Math Skills of Struggling and Reluctant Learners

by
April Duff, M.Ed.
and
Leland Graham, Ph.D.

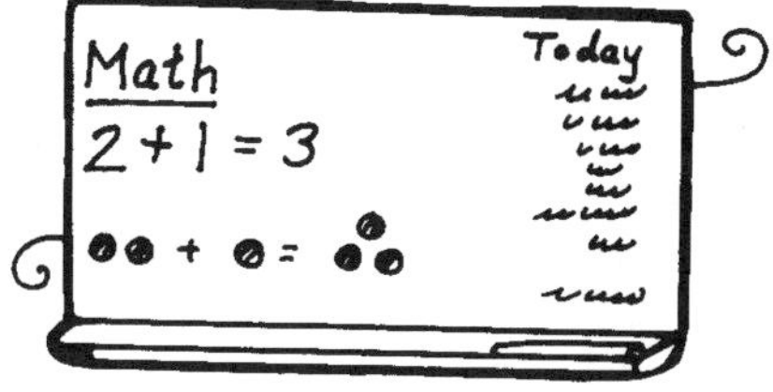

illustrated by
Janet Armbrust

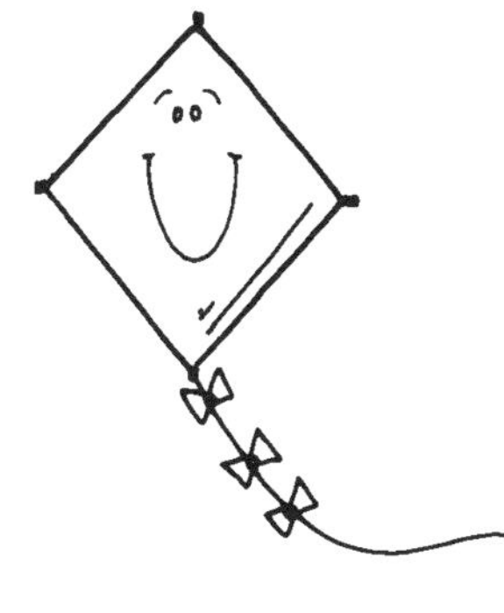

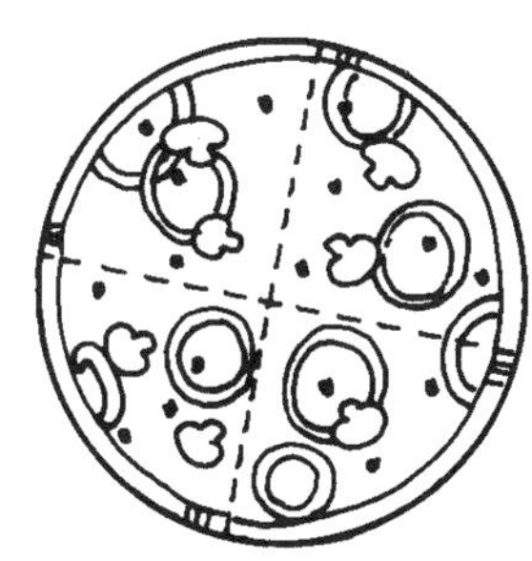

Publisher
Key Education Publishing Company, LLC
Minneapolis, Minnesota

CONGRATULATIONS ON YOUR PURCHASE OF A KEY EDUCATION PRODUCT!

The editors at Key Education are former teachers who bring experience, enthusiasm, and quality to each and every product. Thousands of teachers have looked to the staff at Key Education for new and innovative resources to make their work more enjoyable and rewarding. Key Education is committed to developing and publishing educational materials that will assist teachers in building a strong and developmentally appropriate curriculum for young children.

PLAN FOR GREAT TEACHING EXPERIENCES WHEN YOU USE EDUCATIONAL MATERIALS FROM KEY EDUCATION PUBLISHING COMPANY, LLC

Credits
Authors: April Duff, M.Ed. and Leland Graham, Ph.D.
Publisher: Sherrill B. Flora
Illustrator: Janet Armbrust
Editors: Diane Folkerts
Audrey Rose
George C. Flora
Cover Design: Mary Claire
Production: Swan Johnson

Special Acknowledgement

The authors would like to gratefully acknowledge the assistance and suggestions of the following educators: Jean Anderson and Barry Doran, Math Coordinators from DeKalb County School System, Decatur, Georgia.

Key Education welcomes manuscripts and product ideas from teachers. For a copy of our submission guidelines, please send a self-addressed, stamped envelope to:

Key Education, LLC
Acquisitions Department
9601 Newton Avenue South
Minneapolis, Minnesota 55431

About the Authors

Dr. Leland Graham is a former college professor, principal, and teacher, who was twice voted "Outstanding Teacher of the Year." The author of 55 educational books, Dr. Graham is a popular speaker and workshop presenter throughout Georgia and the USA, as well as a presenter for NSSEA (National School Supply & Equipment Association). Thousands of teachers have benefited from his workshops on reading, phonics, math, and improving achievement scores.

April Duff is a Literacy Support teacher for Even Start in Burke County, Georgia. She has a M.Ed. in Reading, Language and Literacy Education from Georgia State University and a B.S in Early Childhood Education from Georgia College and State University. She has also taught fourth grade, kindergarten and served as an EIP Reading and Math Specialist for grades 1-5. Ms. Duff is a native Atlantan and enjoys reading and traveling.

Standard Book Number: 1-933052-14-7
Keys to Math Success—Grades K–1

Table of Contents

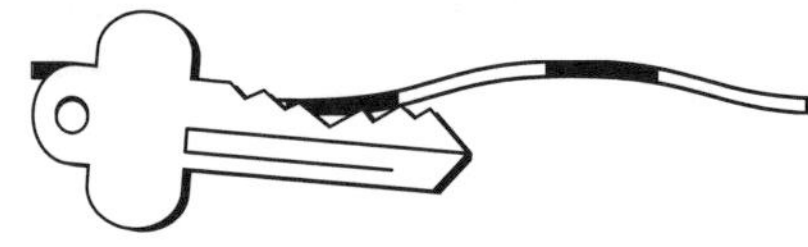

Introduction

Welcome to the *Keys to Math Success* series! Each resource book found in this series is designed to boost and reinforce math skills. All of the included math activities, games, and puzzles will provide good practice for all students, but will be especially useful for those students who are struggling, slightly below average, or for those students who do not seem to be interested in math. The activities will engage these young learners and help them to discover that math can really be fun!

Teachers and parents will find that the presentation of the activities will also help students to succeed. There is some repetition of skills, which reinforces learning; the reproducible activity pages are not overly crowded with too many math problems, which can frustrate students; and the concepts are presented in a clear and student-friendly format. This will make learning about math concepts a fun and successful experience for the children!

Each book offers questions and activities based on the curriculum standards specified by the National Council of Teachers of Mathematics (NCTM). All of the content standards (number and operations, algebra, geometry, measurement, and data analysis and probability) and the process standard of problem solving are incorporated in the activities. At the conclusion of each chapter is a math posttest. Each test has questions and problems that are based on standardized tests, which will help students gain experience and confidence in testing and will increase test scores.

Keys to Math Success is a wonderful resource that may be used for a variety of purposes, such as independent student or classroom work, or may be used at home with parental involvement. These books will quickly become a treasured resource that will help motivate even the most reluctant of math students!

The following math skills are covered in *Keys to Math Success:*

- addition
- subtraction
- place value
- algebraic thinking
- geometry
- fractions
- measurement
- time
- money
- data analysis
- probability
- problem solving
- test-taking skills

Name ______________________

Down on the Farm

Directions: Look at the pictures and numbers below. Write the number words.

1 one

3 three

2 two

4 four

5 five

1 one ______________________

3 ______________________

2 ______________________

4 ______________________

5 ______________________

Down on the Farm

Directions: Look at the pictures and numbers below. Write the number words.

6 six

8 eight

7 seven

9 nine

10 ten

6 ______________

8 ______________

7 ______________

9 ______________

10 ______________

Name ____________________________

Numbers in a Set

Directions: Draw a line from the number to the matching set.

3

7

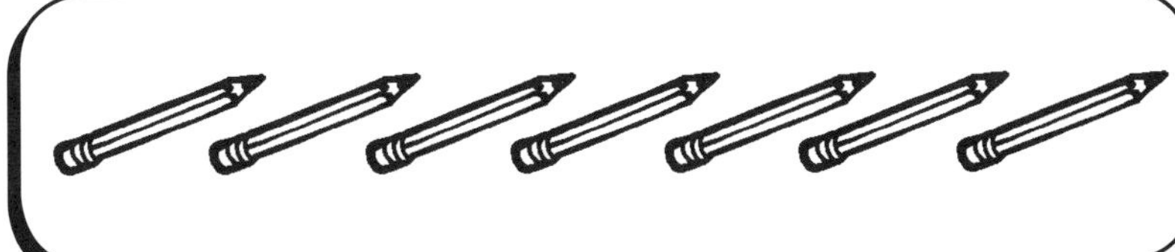

2

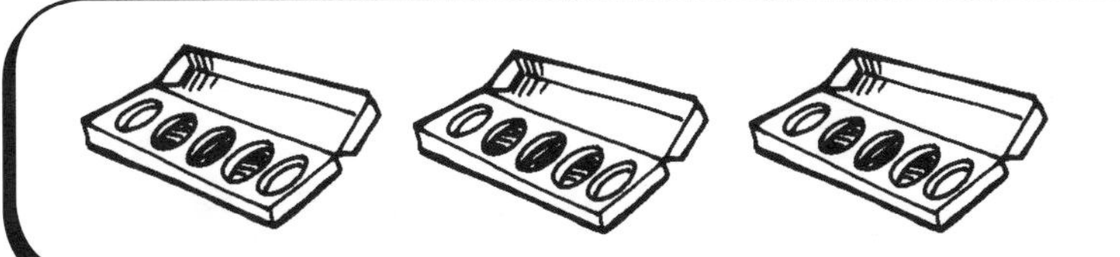

6

4

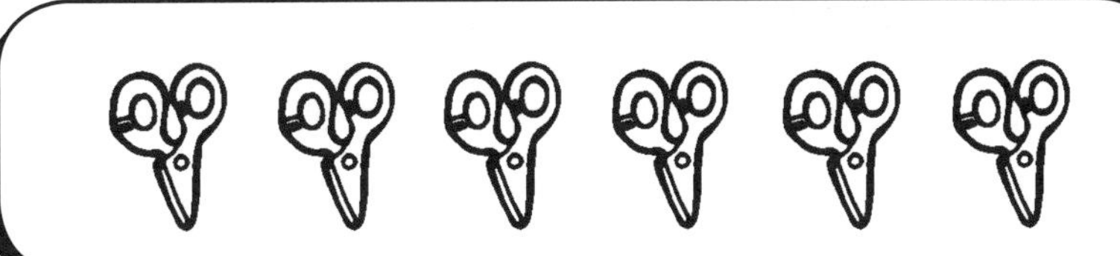

5

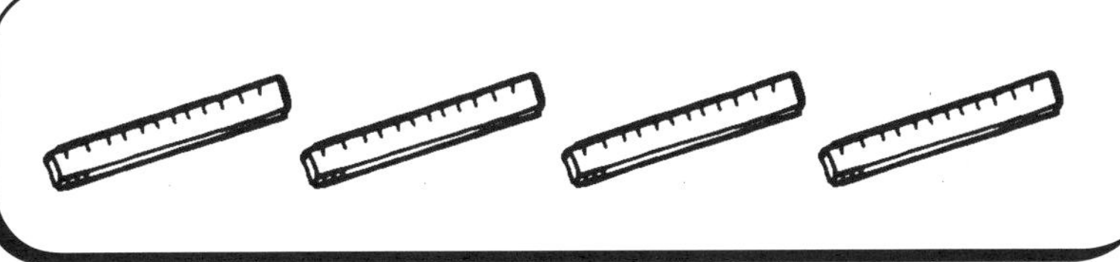

1

Numbers: Cut and Paste

Directions: Cut out the number words at the bottom of the page. Count the dots on the box cars. Match the number words to the number of dots on the box cars. Glue the number words on the matching box cars.

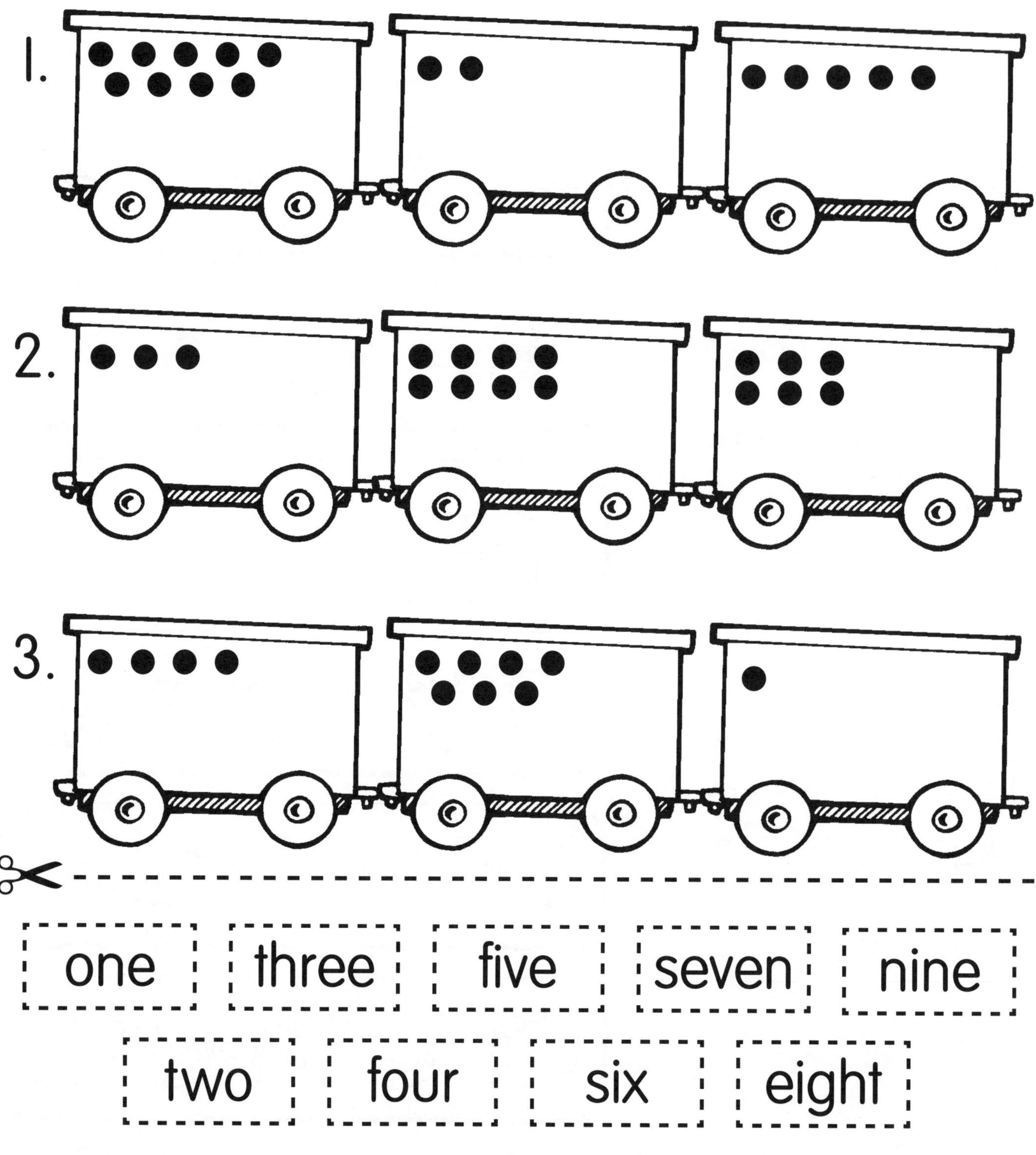

Name ______________________________

Same, Fewer, and More

Example: The cake that is circled has **fewer** candles.

Directions: Circle the cakes with the **same** number of candles.

1.

Directions: Circle the cake with **fewer** candles.

2.

Directions: Circle the cake with **more** candles.

3.

Name ______________________________

What Comes Before, After, or Between?

Directions: Fill in the numbers that are missing on the balloons.

Name ________________________________

Before and After

Directions: What comes **after** the numbers in this row?

1.

Directions: What comes **before** the numbers in this row?

2.

Directions: What comes **before** and **after** the numbers in this row?

3.

Name ______________________________

Let's Count to 100!

Activity ideas are found on page 13.

1	2	3	4	5	6	7	8	9	10
11	12	13	14	15	16	17	18	19	20
21	22	23	24	25	26	27	28	29	30
31	32	33	34	35	36	37	38	39	40
41	42	43	44	45	46	47	48	49	50
51	52	53	54	55	56	57	58	59	60
61	62	63	64	65	66	67	68	69	70
71	72	73	74	75	76	77	78	79	80
81	82	83	84	85	86	87	88	89	90
91	92	93	94	95	96	97	98	99	100

Skip Counting

Note to the Teacher:

The hundreds board on page 12 can be used for many activities. Copy the board for each student and choose from the following activities:

Activity 1 **Even Numbers:** Teach your students that the even numbers are 2, 4, 6, and 8. Color these numbers yellow. Then tell the students that each number that has a 0, 2, 4, 6, or 8 in the ones place is also an even number. Ask the students to help you pick out even numbers. Color as many as you want yellow. You may want to discuss this concept several times. On the first day, stop the lesson at the number 20.

Activity 2 **Odd Numbers:** The odd numbers are 1, 3, 5, 7, and 9. Have the students color the odd numbers orange. Each number that has a 1, 3, 5, 7, or 9 in the ones place is also an odd number. Ask the students to help you pick out the odd numbers. Color as many as you want orange. You may want to continue this activity over several days, so pace yourself accordingly.

Activity 3 **Counting by 5s:** Starting with 5, 10, and 15, count to 100 by 5s with the students. Color these numbers red. Ask the students to count by 5s and identify if the numbers are even or odd, or both. Ask the students to look for patterns on the chart.

Activity 4 **Counting by 10s:** Model counting by 10s for the students. Then have the students repeat the sequence with you several times. Color these numbers blue. Do the students notice anything? All the numbers (10, 20, 30, 40, 50, 60, 70, 80, 90, 100) are already yellow; therefore, they are all even numbers because they have a 0 in the ones place! When they color them blue, the students will have a fun surprise! *(The numbers will turn green.)*

Place Value

Note to the Teacher: Have rods, craft sticks, straws, or anything that can be bundled into sets of 10 available for this activity. The students should complete this activity with manipulatives in conjunction with the worksheet.

Example:

This is a one.

This is a ten rod.

How many tens?

How many ones?

tens	ones
3	5

The number is 35.

1.

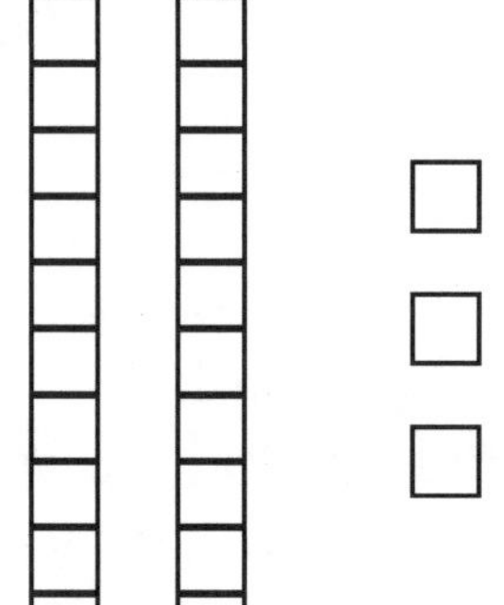

tens	ones

The number is ________.

2.

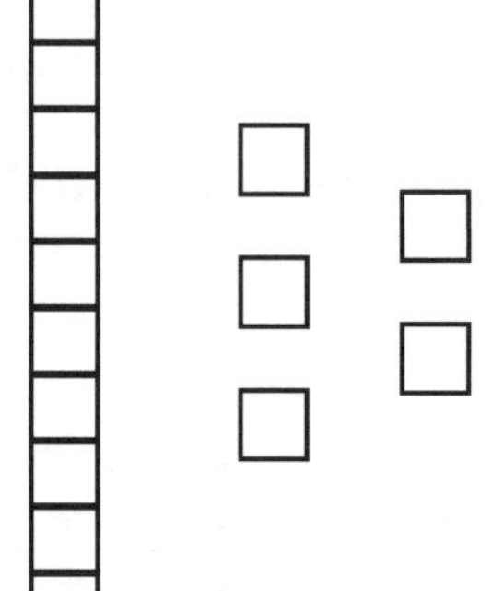

tens	ones

The number is ________.

3.

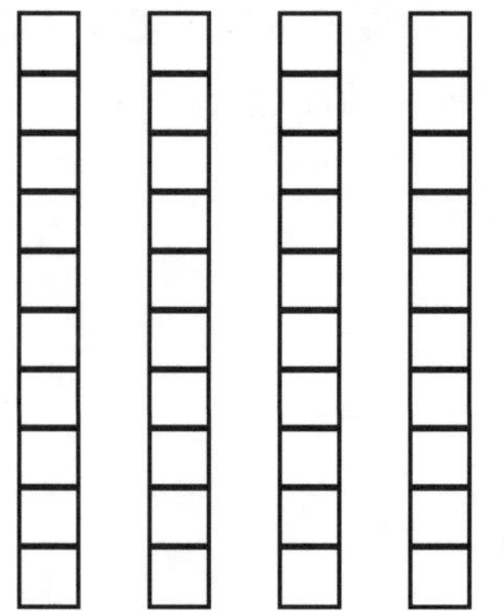

tens	ones

The number is ________.

School of Fish

Directions: The sea creatures are lining up for school! Write the correct ordinal number word for each sea creature that is waiting in line.

Name ______________________________

Combining Sets

Directions: Count the objects and add them together. Write the total on the line.

Example:

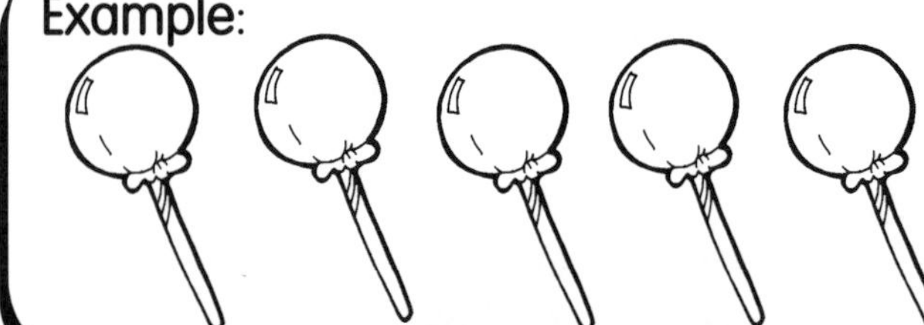 +  = 6

1. 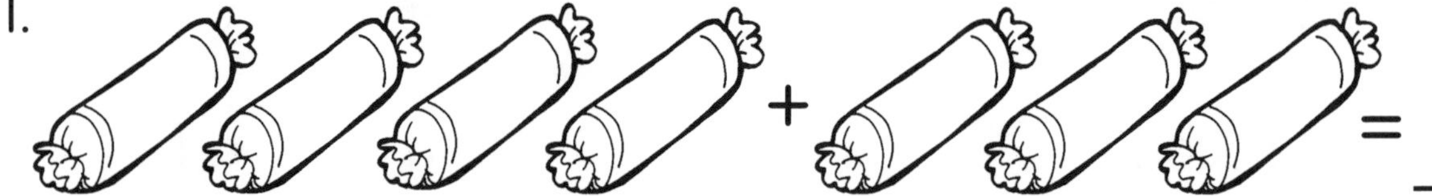 = ______

2.  + 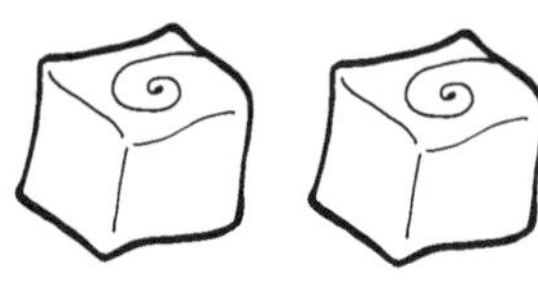 = ______

3.   +  = ______

4. + = ______

5. 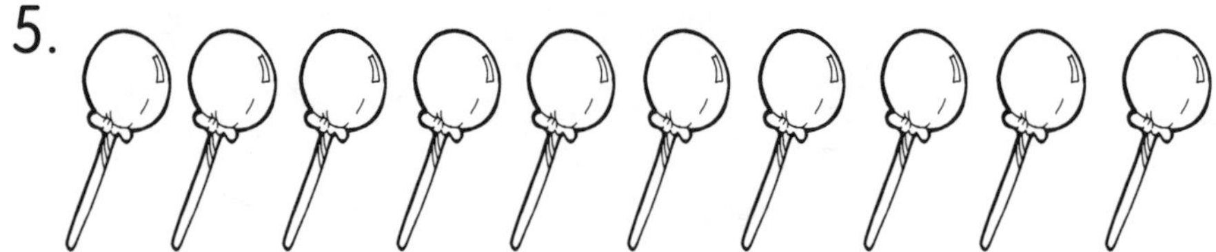 + ____ = ______

Raindrops Keep Adding Up

Directions: Count the raindrops and add them together. Write the number on each umbrella.

Example:

1 + 2 = 3

1. 1 + 2 =

2. 3 + 2 =

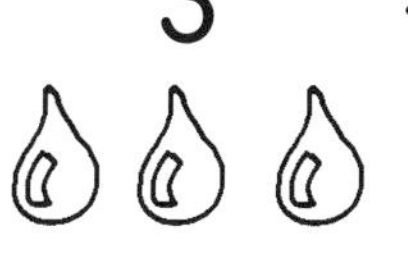

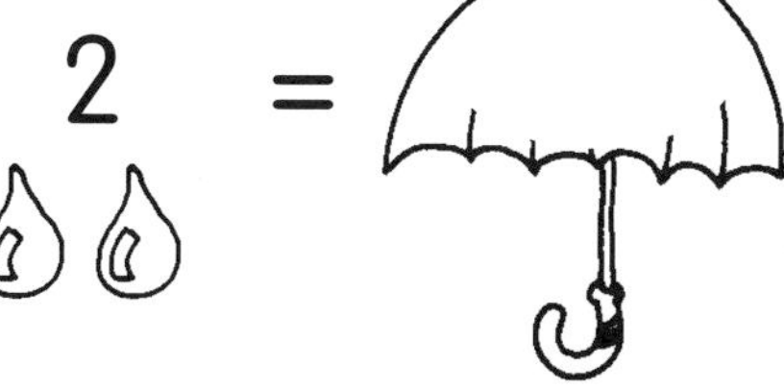

3. 4 + 3 =

4. 5 + 0 =

5. 4 + 5 =

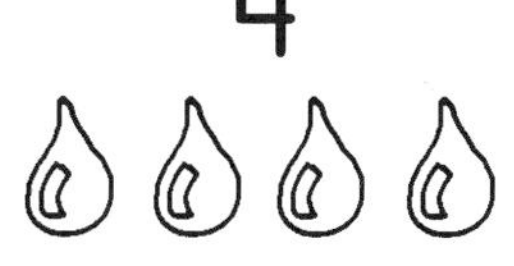

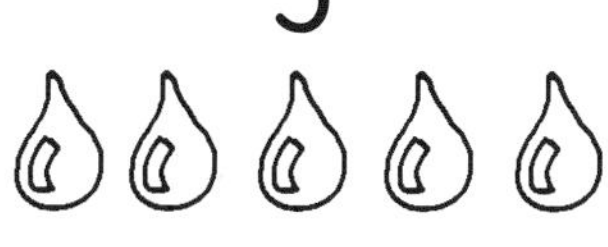

Name ______________________________

Take Away

Directions: Study the example below. Solve each problem. Write the subtraction sentence on the line.

Rule: Subtraction is "taking away" the value of one number from another number to find the difference.

Example:

5	–	3	=	2
How many in the set?	Take away	How many X?		How many left?

1.

____	–	____	=	____
How many in the set?	Take away	How many X?		How many left?

2.

____	–	____	=	____
How many in the set?	Take away	How many X?		How many left?

3.

____	–	____	=	____
How many in the set?	Take away	How many X?		How many left?

Name ___________________________________

More Take Away

Directions: Study the example. Place an X on what is being taken away. Write the answer on each blank.

Example:

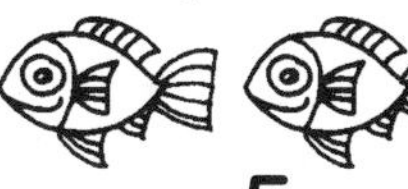

How many X marks will you place? 2

How many are left? 5

7 – 2 = 5

1.  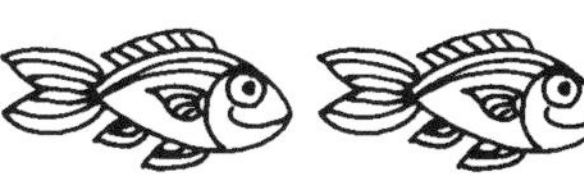 

8 – 4 = ______

2.  

6 – 1 = ______

3.    

4 – 2 = ______

4.    

10 – 4 = ______

5.   

5 – 3 = ______

Homework: Stories with Numbers

Dear Parents,

We have been studying number concepts. The children have been sequencing numbers, skip counting, working with place value, and beginning addition and subtraction. You may want to strengthen your child's understanding of these concepts by reading *Ten Apples Up on Top*, by Dr. Seuss (Beginner Books, Random House, 1988) and *Ten Black Dots*, by Donald Crews (Greenwillow, 1986). Here are some great activities that you can do with your child at home.

Activity 1 Read aloud one of the above-mentioned stories. Have your child echo each of the numbers as you read.

Activity 2 Challenge your child to find different objects in various quantities around the house, such as 5 forks, 3 magazines, 4 cotton balls, 7 crayons, etc.

Activity 3 Write the numbers 1–10 on small slips of paper. Place the numbers in a hat or bowl. Have your child pull out a number. Then have your child draw a silly picture containing that number of items. For example, if your child picks the number 6, he may draw a creature with 6 arms.

Activity 4 Purchase some sidewalk chalk. Then take your child outside to have some fun with addition. Parents, your task is to draw various objects on the sidewalk. Ask your child to use the pictures to write several addition sentences, such as 4 + 3 = 7.

Name ______________________________

Problem Solving

Directions: Solve the following problems.

1. 

If you add 2 more, how many will you have?

______

2. What numbers will come before, between, and after the given numbers?

____ , 13, 14, ____ , ____ ,

17, ____ , 19, 20, ____

3. Circle the number that is in the one's place?

47

4. Draw objects for this addition sentence.

3 + 4 = 7

	+		=	

5. Count the acorns. If a squirrel ate 3,

how many would be left? ______

6. Circle the 2 mittens with the same number of polka dots.

Picture Patterns

Directions: Look at the pictures and the letters under them. Do you see a pattern? Draw pictures to complete the patterns.

Example:

A B A B A B

1. 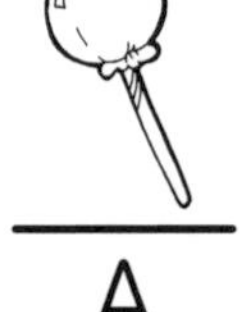

A B A B A B

2.  

A B C A B C

3.  

A B A B A B

4. 

A B B A B B

5.  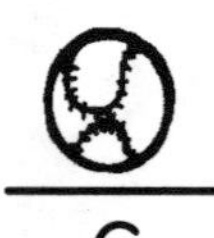

A B C A B C

Name ______________________________

Circles, Rectangles, Stars, Oh My!

Directions: Look at the shapes. Do you see the pattern? Complete the pattern.

Example:

 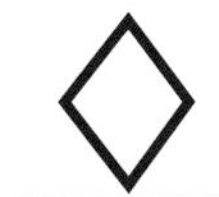    

1.      ______

2. ______     ______ ______

3. ______    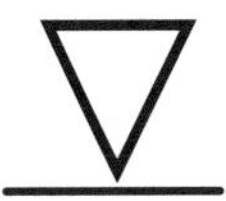 ______ ______

4.   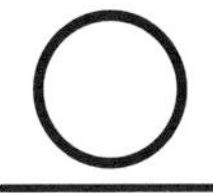 ______ ______ ______

5. 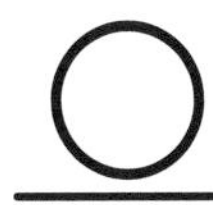  ______ ______

6. 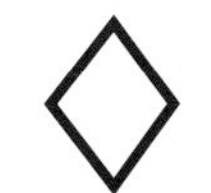 ______  ______ 

Name ______________________________

Patterning: Cut and Paste

Directions: Cut out the pictures at the bottom of the page.
Glue the pictures in the correct row to complete each pattern.

1.  ____________  ____________ 

2.   

3. ____________  ____________

Name ________________________________

What's the Missing Number?

Directions: Look at the number patterns.
Write the missing number on each line to complete the pattern.

1. 2 3 4 2 3 ____

2. 4 5 6 4 ____ 6

3. 8 7 6 ____ 7 6

4. 6 9 6 9 ____ 9

5. 1 3 5 1 ____ 5

6. 0 1 1 ____ 1 1

Name ______________________

The Shape of Numbers

Directions: Each shape represents a specific number. Complete the problems below.

3 + △ = 7 △ + ○ = 9 1. What is △? ____ 2. What is ○? ____	1 + □ = 6 □ + ♡ = 7 5. What is □? ____ 6. What is ♡? ____
4 + □ = 8 □ + ◇ = 5 3. What is □? ____ 4. What is ◇? ____	2 + ☆ = 3 ☆ + ○ = 10 7. What is ☆? ____ 8. What is ○? ____

Do They Match?

Directions: Match the addition sentences in Column A to the sets in Column B.
Look carefully! The numbers may be turned around.

Example:

2 + 3 = ♡♡ + ♡♡♡

3 + 2 = ♡♡♡ + ♡♡

Column A	Column B
1. 6 + 0 = 6	a.
2. 1 + 4 =	b.
3. 5 + 4 =	c.
4. 7 + 1 =	d.
5. 2 + 8 =	e.

Name ________________________________

How Did It Change?

Note to the Teacher: Two concepts in algebra are qualitative change and quantitative change. **Qualitative change** can be described as objects becoming taller, colder, or heavier. **Quantitative change** can be measured through the use of measurement tools such as scales, thermometers, or rulers. One way to present these ideas to young children is to discuss objects that they can actually see change, such as seeds becoming plants or bread becoming toast.

Directions: Read the book *The Very Hungry Caterpillar,* by Eric Carle, (Philomel Books, 1987). Discuss with the students how the caterpillar changes (it grows fatter day by day; at last, it turns into a butterfly). Complete the following matching activity with your class.

Name ____________________________________

Classroom Sorting

Directions: Draw pictures of the **Word Bank** objects in the table below. For example, draw counters under math. Encourage the children to draw their own ideas.

Word Bank:

books	computer	picture	paper
audiotapes	scissors	crayons	teddy bear counters
paints	clock	ruler	pencil

1. Reading	2. Writing	3. Math	4. Art

Homework: Grocery-Store Sorting

Dear Parents,

In this section we have been studying algebraic concepts such as patterning and sorting. You may want to strengthen your child's understanding of these concepts by reading *Big Dog, Little Dog,* by Philip D. Eastman (Random House, 1973) or *The Three Billy Goats Gruff,* by Paul Galdone (Clarion, 1973). Here are some fun activities that will reinforce your child's learning.

Activity 1 Go grocery shopping! Have your child choose products that come in an assortment of containers, such as bags, boxes, and cans. Ask your child to tell you if the item is in a bag, a box, or in a can.

Activity 2 Now, help your child sort each type of container (bags, boxes, and cans) by size, such as small, medium, or large. Ask your child to explain why she chose to describe the item as small, medium, or large.

Activity 3 When you and your child return home, complete the chart below. Help your child to decide into which category each item should be placed and then draw a picture of that item.

Bags	Boxes	Cans

Name ______________________________

Problem Solving

Directions: Solve the following problems.

1. Complete the pattern.

2. Are they equal? Circle **yes** or **no**.

A. 2 + 3 =

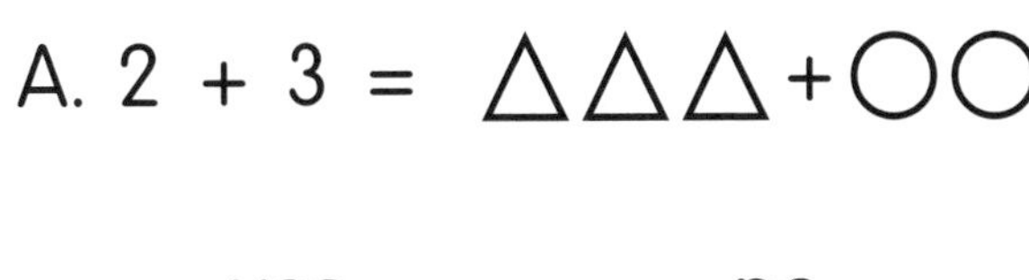

yes **no**

B. 4 + 2 = ♡♡♡ + ♡♡♡

yes **no**

C. □ + ☆☆☆☆☆ = 5 + 1

yes **no**

3.

3 + □ = 7

□ + △ = 7

A. What is □ ? ____

B. What is △ ? ____

4. Which object below became a tree? Circle the correct answer.

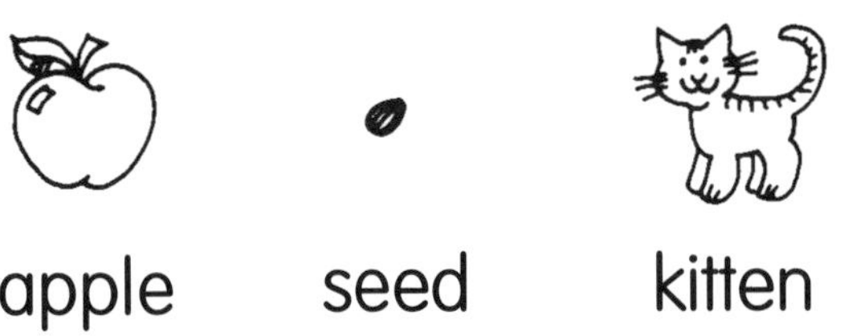

apple seed kitten

5. What numbers are missing?

____, 38, 39, ____, ____, 42

6. Sort the following shapes by size.

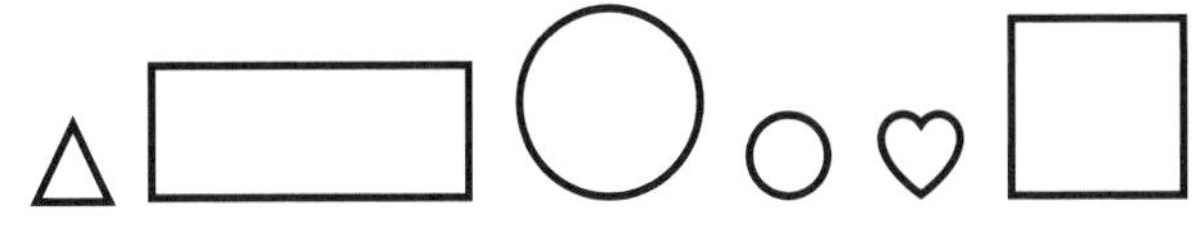

small	large

Circles and Ovals

A **circle** ◯ is a round shape.

Trace the circles.

1. Color the objects that are in the shape of a circle. ______________________

2. Draw 5 circles of your own here. ______________________

An **oval** ⬯ is a round shape, but it is longer than a circle.

Trace the ovals.

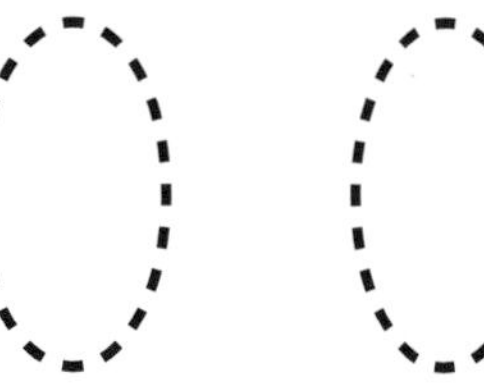

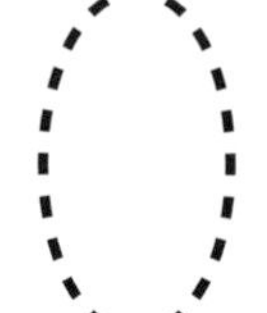

3. Color the objects that are in the shape of an oval. ______________________

4. Draw 5 ovals of your own here. ______________________

Name ______________________________

Squares, Rectangles, and Triangles

A **square** ☐ has 4 sides. All sides are the same length.

Trace the squares.

1. Color the objects that are in the shape of a square.

A **rectangle** ▭ also has 4 sides. 2 sides are short and 2 sides are long.

Trace the **rectangles**.

2. Draw 4 objects with a rectangular shape.

A **triangle** △ has 3 sides. The sides can be the same length.

Trace the triangles.

3. Color the objects that are in the shape of a triangle.

Diamonds, Stars, and Hearts

A **diamond** ◇ has 4 sides like a square, but it is turned on its point.

Trace the diamonds.

1. Draw 5 diamonds here. ______________________

A **star** ☆ is a special shape.

Trace the stars.

2. Draw 5 stars here. ______________________

A **heart** ♡ is also a special shape.

Trace the hearts.

3. Draw 5 hearts here. ______________________

Name ______________________________

Is It a Shape?

Directions: Look at each picture. Is it a shape we have studied? Circle **yes** or **no**.

1.
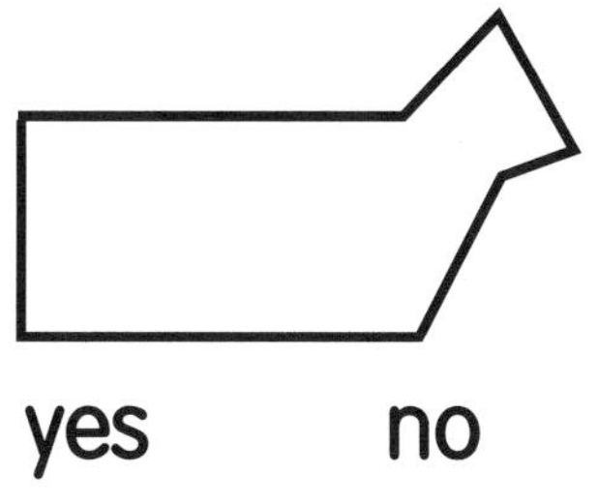
yes no

6.

yes no

2.

yes no

7.

yes no

3.
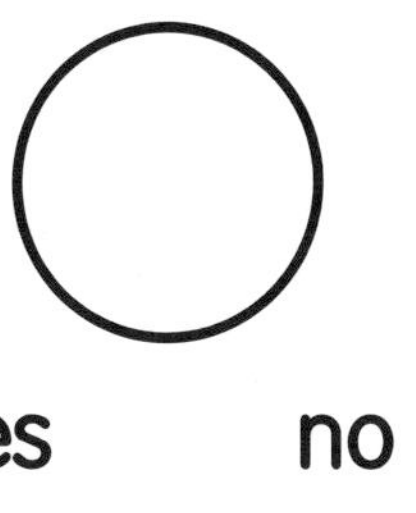
yes no

8.
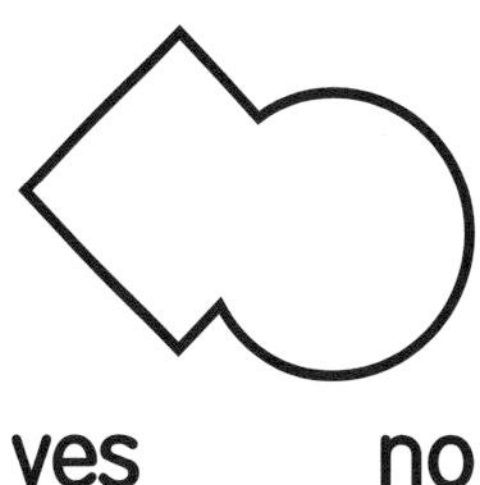
yes no

4.
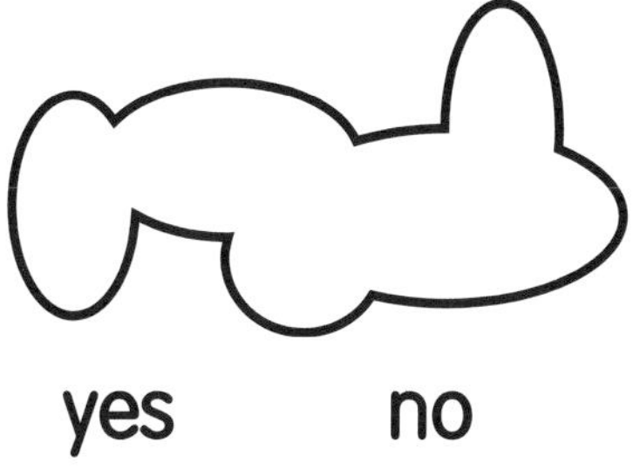
yes no

9.
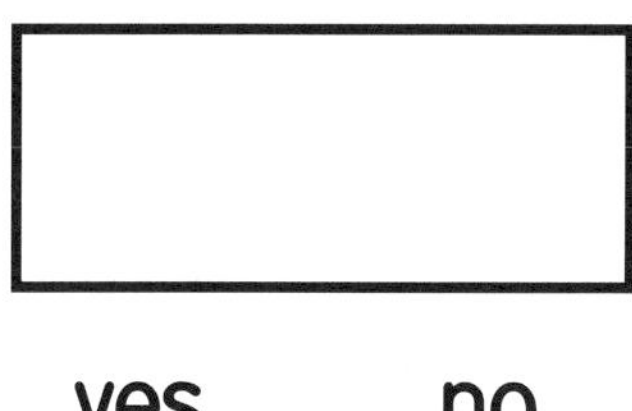
yes no

5.
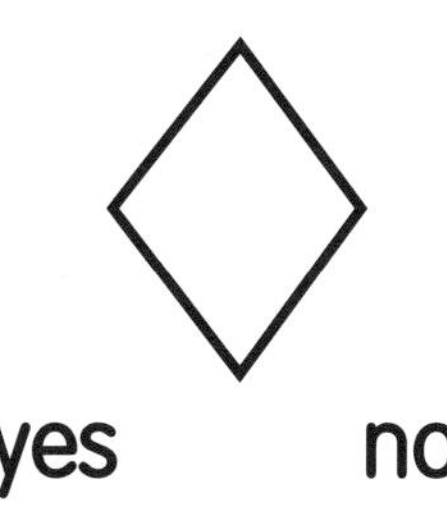
yes no

10.
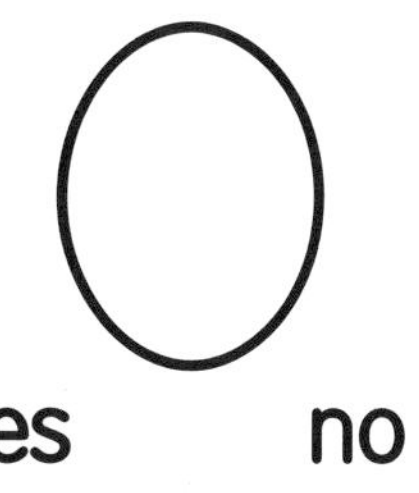
yes no

Larger Than, Smaller Than

Explanation: When one object is larger than another object, we say it is **larger than**. When one object is smaller than another object, we say it is **smaller than**.

Directions: Look at each row below. Is the object in Column A **larger than** or **smaller than** the object in Column B? The first one has been done for you.

	Column A			Column B
1.	○	is		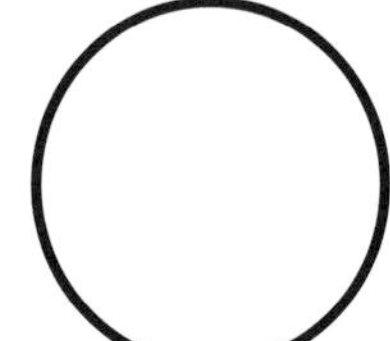
2.		is	______________	
3.		is	______________	
4.		is	______________	
5.	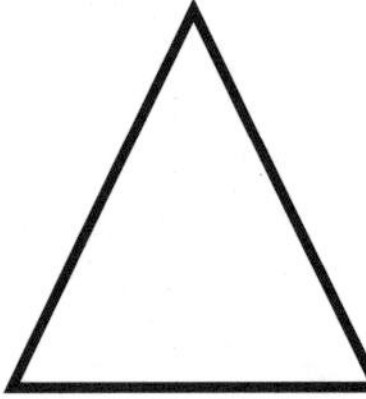	is	______________	

Name ______________________________

Shapes: Cut and Paste

Directions: Use the shapes on the next page to add buildings, signs, and other objects to the city.

XYZ ING

BOOKS

Shapes to cut out and paste for page 37.

Name ______________________

Split Down the Middle

Explanation: If you fold an object in half and it is the same on both sides, that object is said to have **symmetry**.

Directions: Look at each picture below. Does it show symmetry? Circle **yes** or **no**. The first one has been done for you.

1.

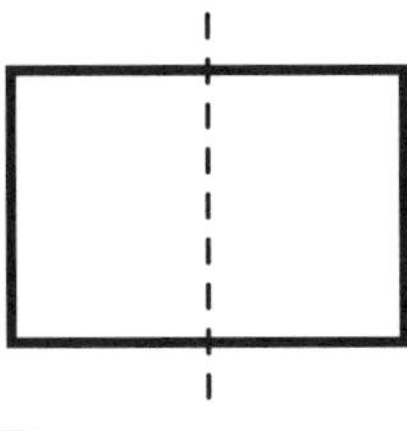

(yes) no

2.

yes no

3.

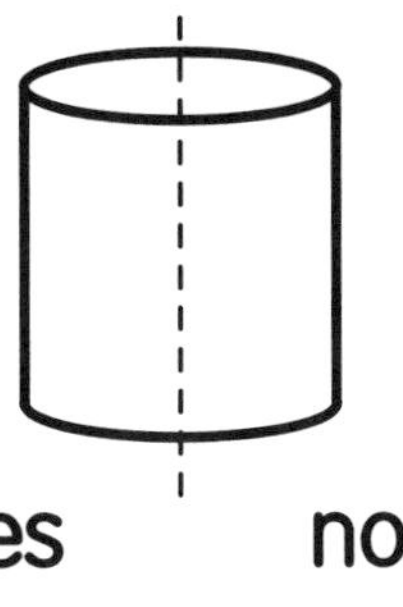

yes no

4.

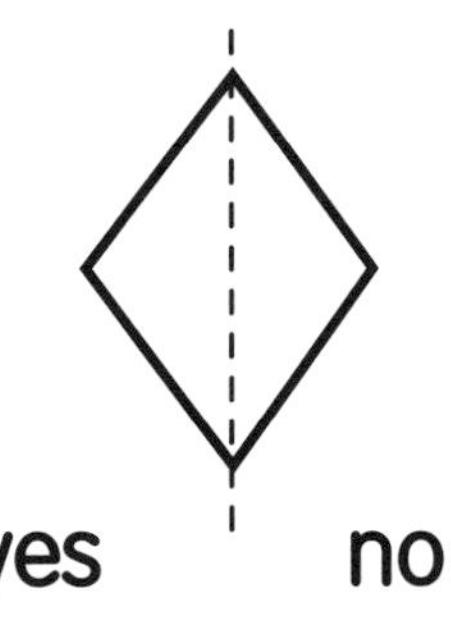

yes no

5.

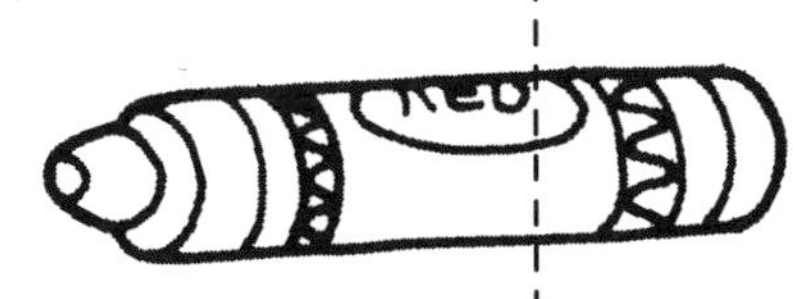

yes no

6.

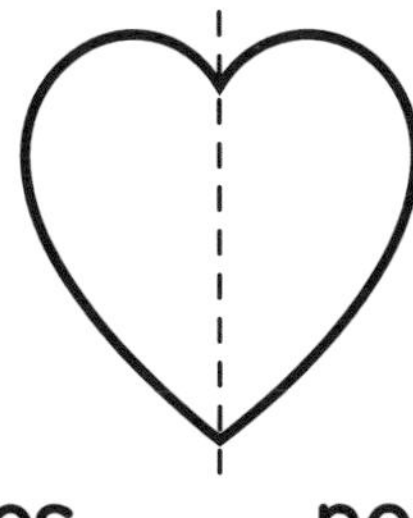

yes no

7.

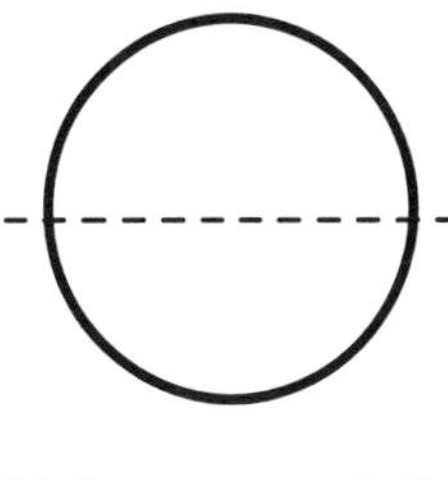

yes no

8.

yes no

Shapes All Around Us!

Directions: Write the name of the shape.
Match the shape to the object that also has the same shape.

Word Bank

circle square triangle diamond rectangle

1. ______________________

2. ______________________

3. ______________________

4. ______________________

5. ______________________

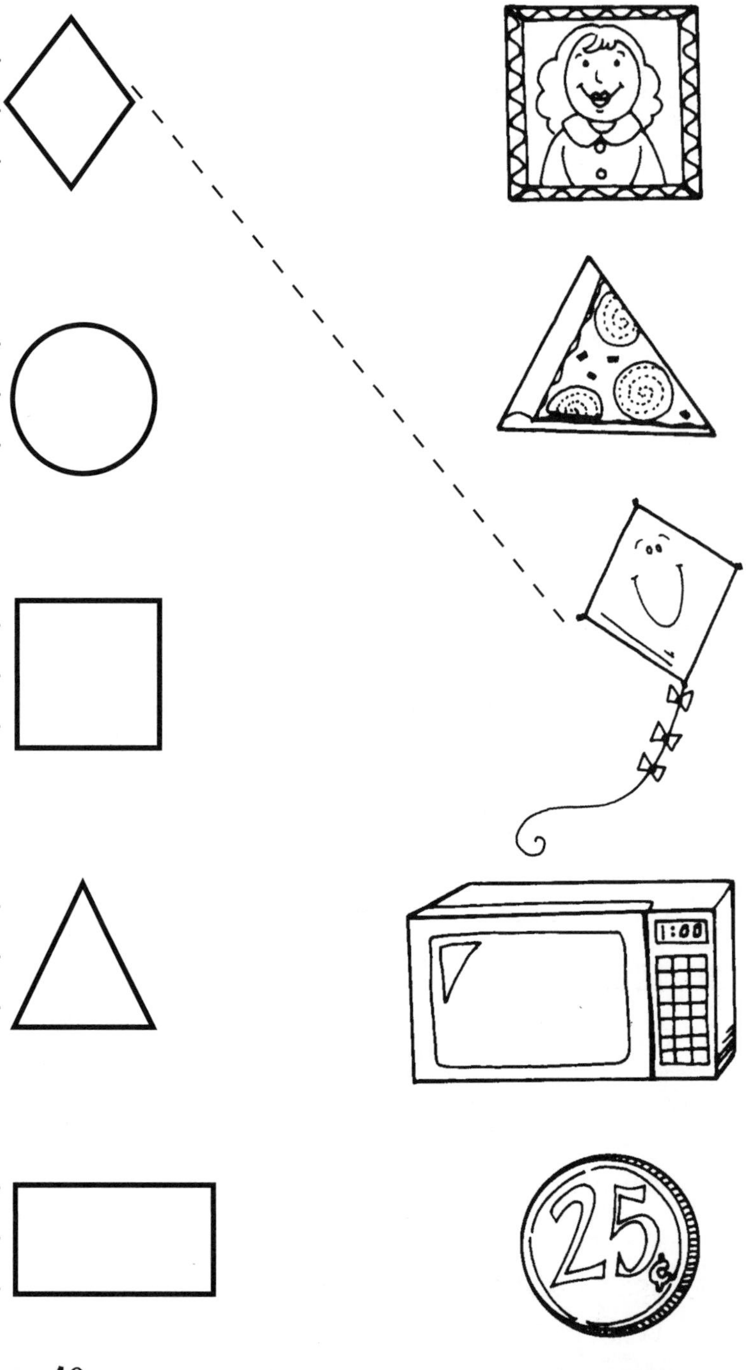

Lisa's Looking for Her Instrument!

Lisa is performing in a concert today. She is carrying an instrument in her hands. Complete the activity and find out what instrument Lisa plays.

Directions: Look at the graph. Fill in the blanks with the correct answer. The first one has been done for you.

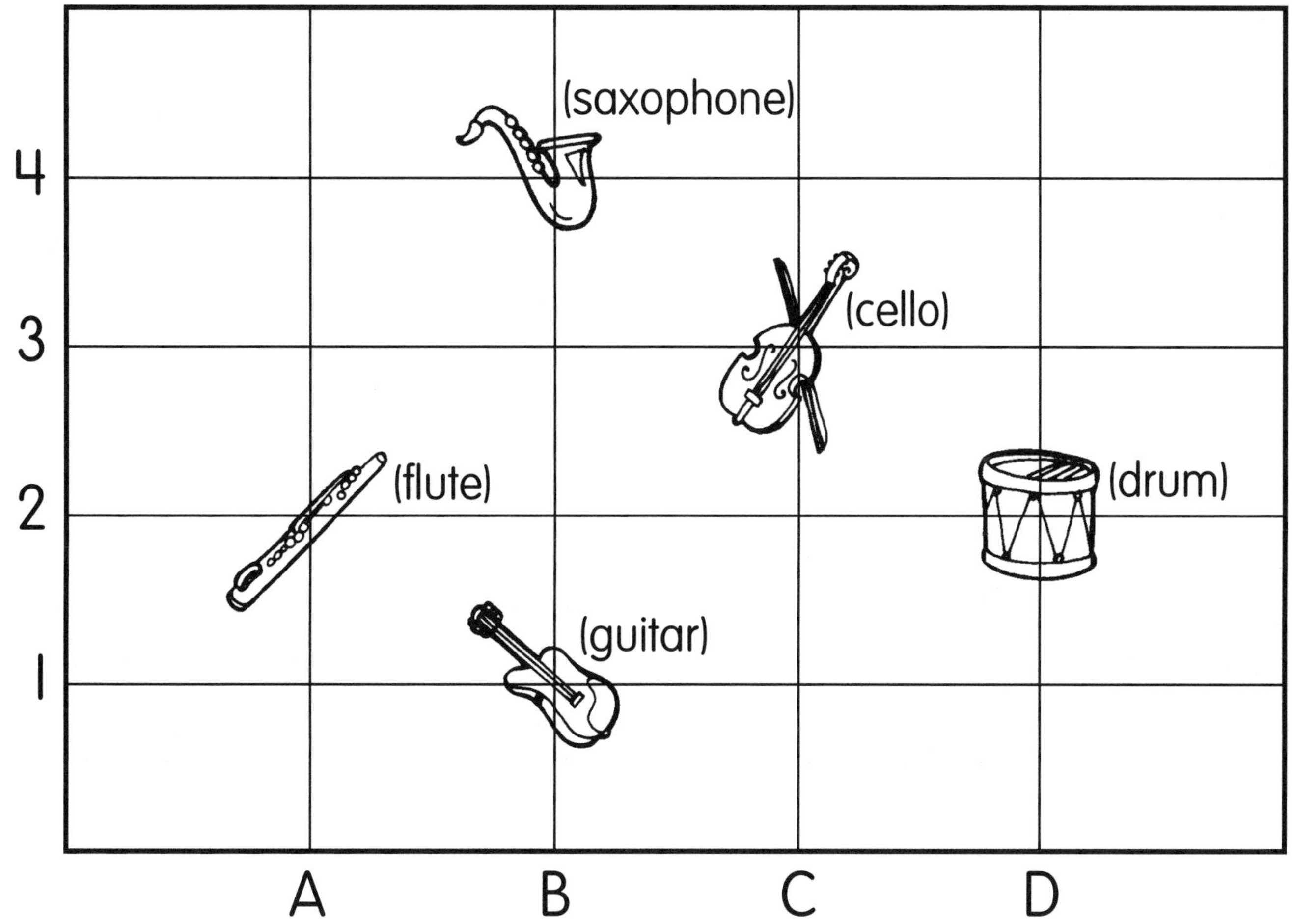

1. What instrument is at B1? guitar
2. Where is the saxophone? ______________________.
3. What instrument is at A2? ______________________
4. Lisa's instrument is at D2. What is it? ______________________

Positions in the Garden

Directions: Study the picture below. Circle the correct position words.

1. The butterfly is (**above** , **below**) the flowers.
2. The worm is (**over** , **under**) the tree.
3. The bird is to the (**left** , **right**) of the flowers.
4. The kite is to the (**left** , **right**) in the sky.
5. The snail is (**near** , **far from**) the flowers.

Homework: Shoe Box and Bear

Dear Parents,

We have been learning about geometry, including the use of positional words (inside/outside, behind/in front of, over/under). You may want to increase your child's understanding of these concepts by reading either *Shapes in Nature,* by Judy Feldman (Children's Press, 1991) or *Changes, Changes,* by Pat Hutchins (Macmillan, 1987). Below are some fun activities to do with your child to reinforce geometrical concepts.

Activity 1 Find a shoe box and a teddy bear. Discuss with your child a variety of positional words (on, in, off, beside, etc.). Write each positional word on an index card. Mix up the cards. Hold a card up and read the word with your child. Have your child place the teddy bear in relation to the shoe box to illustrate the positional word written on the card.

Activity 2 Ask your child to listen to the following directions that you will give in order to complete a picture in the box below: 1) Draw a square. 2) Draw a triangle on top of the square. 3) Draw a rectangle inside the square. 4) Draw a flower to the right of the square. 5) Draw a dog or cat to the left of the square. 6) Draw several clouds above the square.

Problem Solving

Directions: Solve the following problems.

1. I have 4 sides. All 4 sides are not the same length. What am I? Draw me here.

4. On another sheet of paper, draw a picture using only these shapes:

2. Color the **circle red**. Color the **oval blue**. Color the **star yellow**.

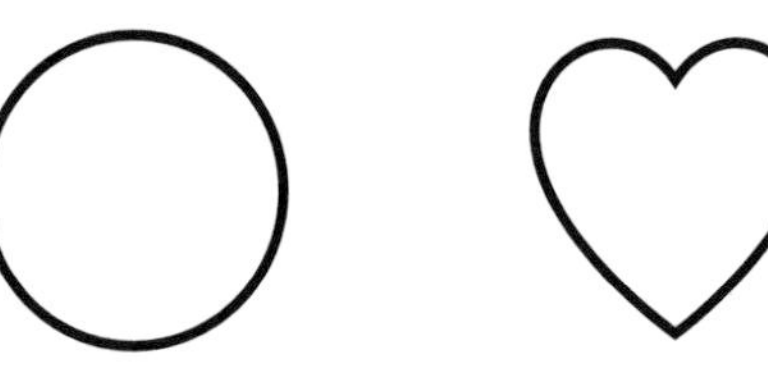

5. Find a number that is inside the rectangle but outside the circle. It is also inside the square.

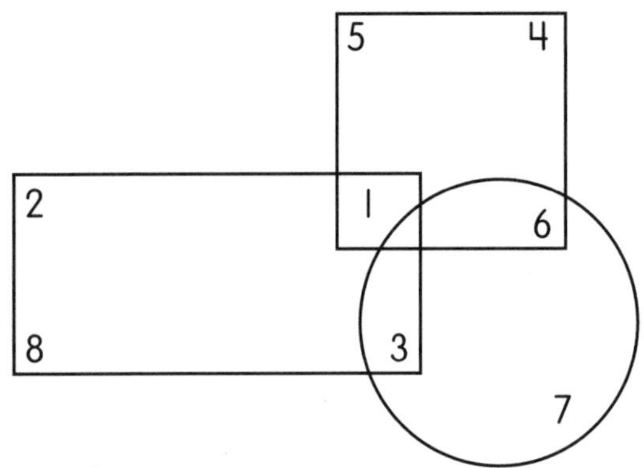

The number is ______.

3. Draw a line of symmetry so that both sides will be the same.

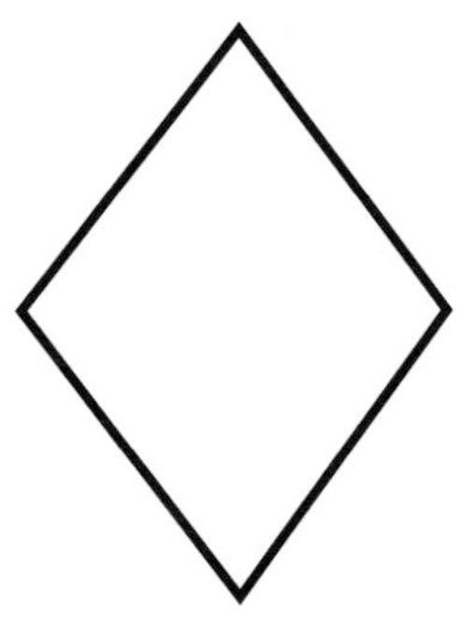

6. Your favorite food is a slice of pizza. Draw the shape of a slice of pizza.

Name ______________________________

Share and Share Alike

Directions: Cut out the keys. Glue them in the boxes.
Each box in the same row should have the same number of keys.

1.

2.

3.

Simone Shares Her Snacks
(Halves and Wholes)

Sometimes Simone has a whole snack all to herself. She does not have to share it.
This is Simone's **whole** cookie. 

On Fridays, Simone's friend Gerry comes over. Simone has to share her cookie with Gerry.

When Simone shares, she breaks her cookie in **half** ($\frac{1}{2}$).

This is Simone's half cookie. ⟶ ⟵ This is Gerry's half.

Directions: Look at the following pictures. Is Simone sharing a snack with Gerry or does she have the whole snack? Circle **whole** or **half**.

1. whole half	4. whole half
2. whole half	5. whole half
3. whole half	6. whole half

Simone Shares Again!
(Fourths)

It is Saturday. Simone is having a party. Gerry, Mike, and Julie are coming to her party. Simone will share her treats with her three friends.

The treat is cut into **fourths** ($\frac{1}{4}$).

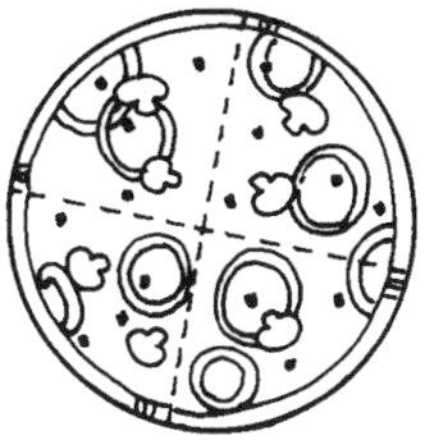

Directions: Look at the following pictures. Did Simone cut her treats into **fourths**? Circle **yes** or **no**.

1. yes no	3. yes no
2. yes no	4. yes no

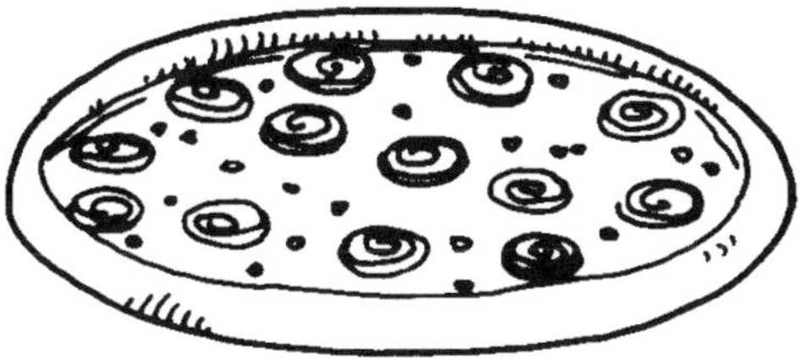

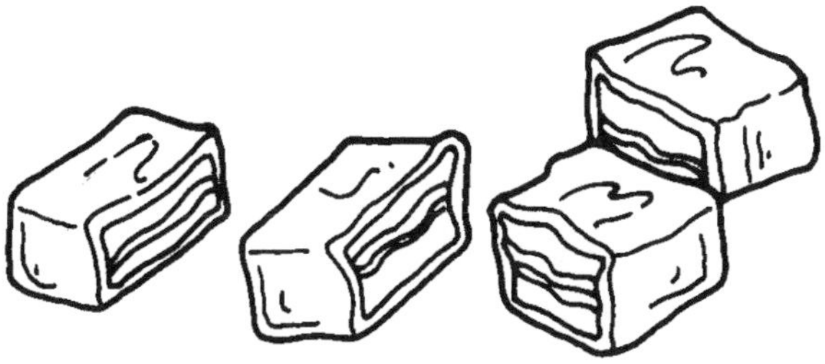

Name ____

Three Cheers for Simone
(Thirds)

It is Sunday. Simone is spending the day with her sister, Suzanne, and Grandma Shirley. Grandma Shirley cuts snacks in **thirds** for the three of them to share.

One cookie would look like this:  ($\frac{1}{3}$).

Directions: Look at the following pictures. Did Grandma Shirley cut the treat into **thirds**? Circle **yes** or **no**.

1. **yes** **no**	3. **yes** **no**
2. **yes** **no**	4. **yes** **no**

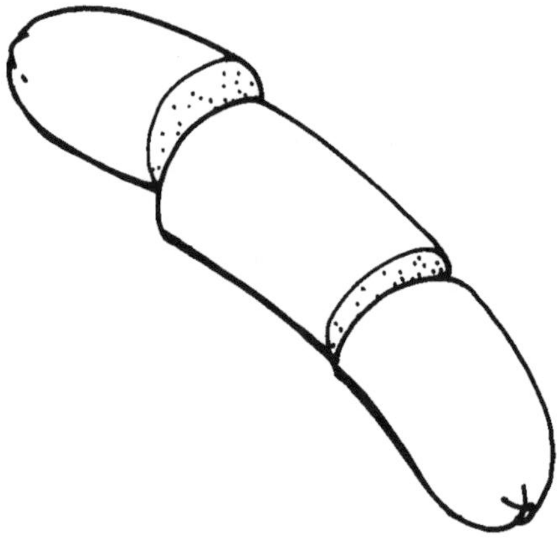

Name ______________________________

Cut and Paste: Fractions 1, $\frac{1}{2}$, $\frac{1}{4}$, $\frac{1}{3}$

Directions: Look at the shapes below. Is the whole shape shaded or is the shape shaded to show halves ($\frac{1}{2}$), thirds ($\frac{1}{3}$), or fourths ($\frac{1}{4}$)? Cut out the correct fraction for each shaded shape. Glue the fraction that shows what part is shaded in the circle.

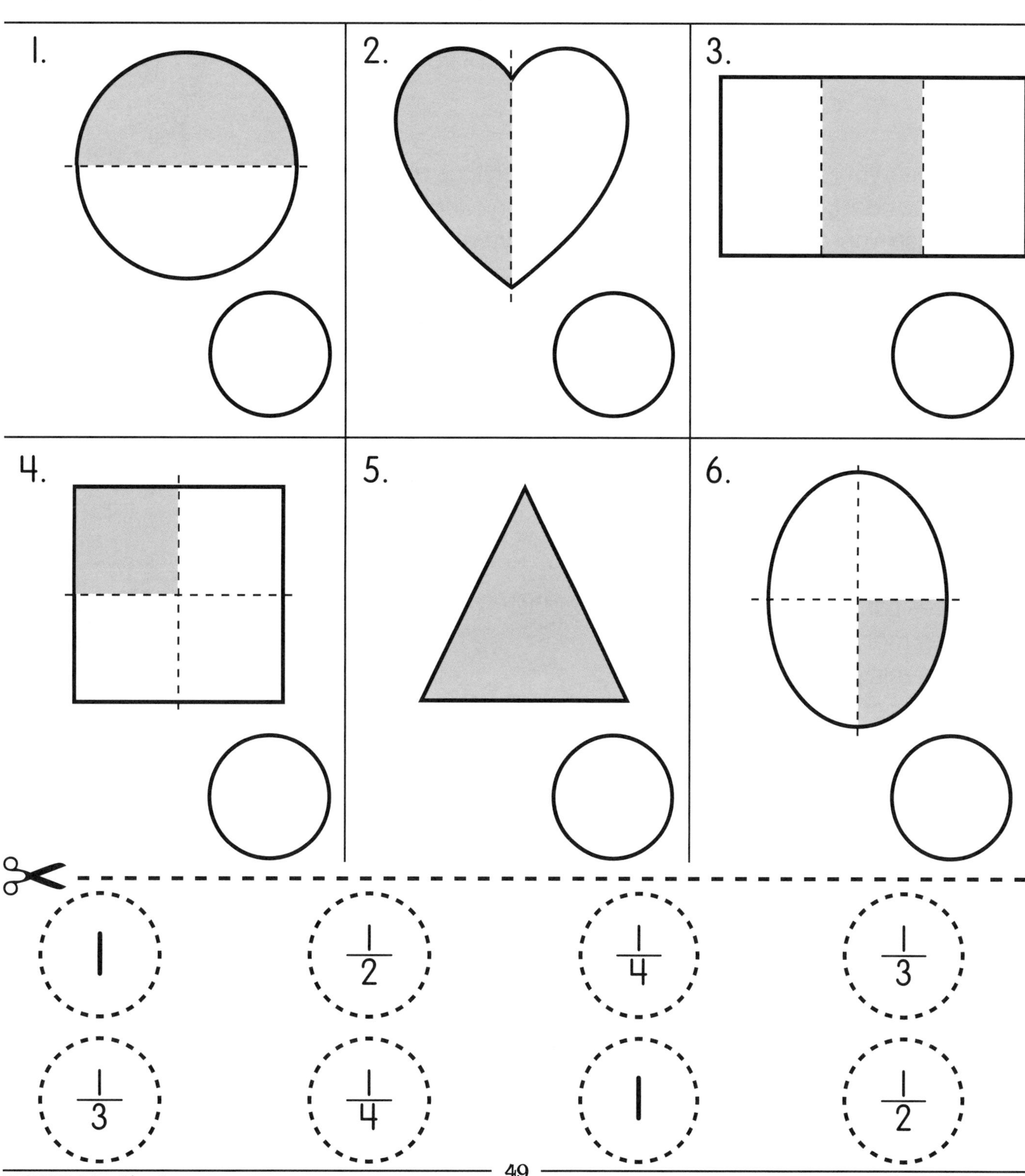

1 $\frac{1}{2}$ $\frac{1}{4}$ $\frac{1}{3}$

$\frac{1}{3}$ $\frac{1}{4}$ 1 $\frac{1}{2}$

Homework: Ambrosia Adventure

Dear Parents,

We have been learning about fractions. You may want to further your child's studies by reading *Fractions Are Parts of Things*, by Richard J. Dennis (T.Y. Crowell, 1971) or *Eating Fractions,* by Bruce McMillan (Scholastic, 1991). Here is a fun activity to do with your child at home to reinforce the concept of fractions.

Activity

Talk with your child about cooking. Tell her that almost all recipes include fractions! Find a cookbook and look through it for a dish you can cook together. You may want to try the following recipe.

Ambrosia Salad

Utensils needed: butter knife, bowl, measuring cups, and spoons

Ingredients:

- 1/2 banana
- 2 slices canned pineapple (cut into fourths)
- 1/4 cup mandarin oranges, drained
- 1/3 cup miniature marshmallows
- 2 tablespoons vanilla yogurt
- 2 teaspoons coconut flakes

Directions:

1. Slice the banana into small pieces and place in a bowl.
2. Add the pineapple and mandarin oranges. Mix gently.
3. Spoon in the vanilla yogurt and stir all together.
4. Sprinkle the marshmallows and coconut flakes on top.
5. Serve and enjoy.

Note to the Teacher: Cut a piece of string 6 inches in length for each student or each pair of students. Tell them to find and then measure the classroom objects pictured below. Have them circle whether the object is **Longer** or **Shorter** than the string.

Name ____________________

Problem Solving

Directions: Solve the following problems.

1. With how many friends could Jay share this pizza with equally? Hint: Remember to count Jay!

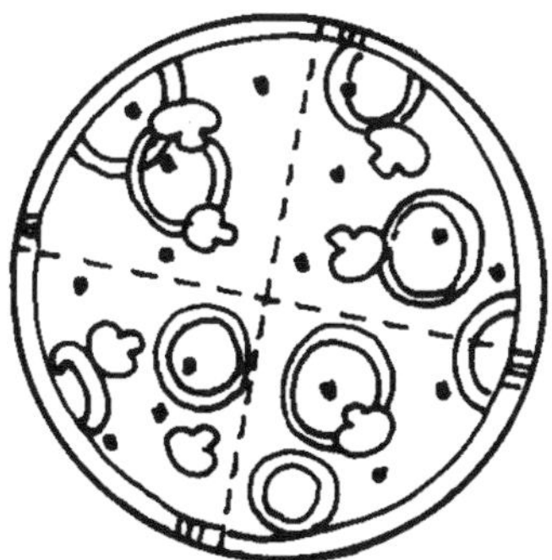

A. 2

B. 3

C. 4

2. Color $\frac{1}{2}$ of the square blue. Color $\frac{1}{4}$ of the square yellow.

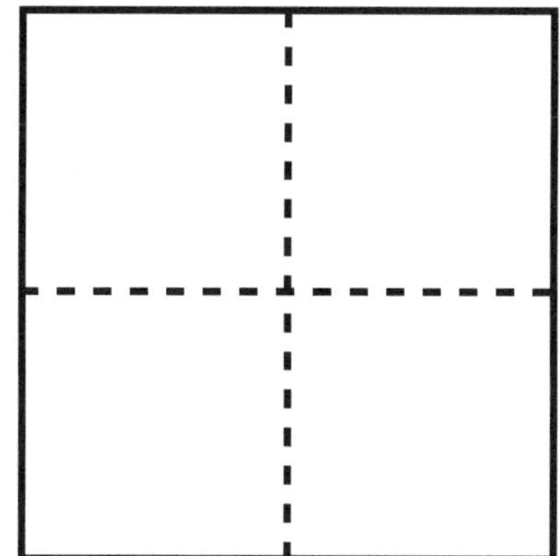

3. What part of this cookie has been eaten?

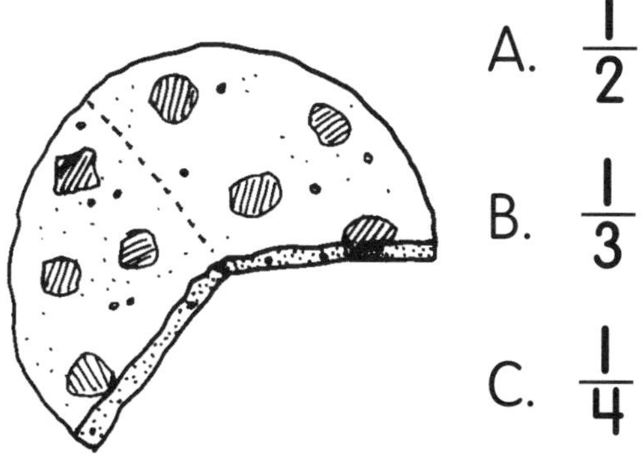

A. $\frac{1}{2}$

B. $\frac{1}{3}$

C. $\frac{1}{4}$

4. What fraction of this triangle is shaded?

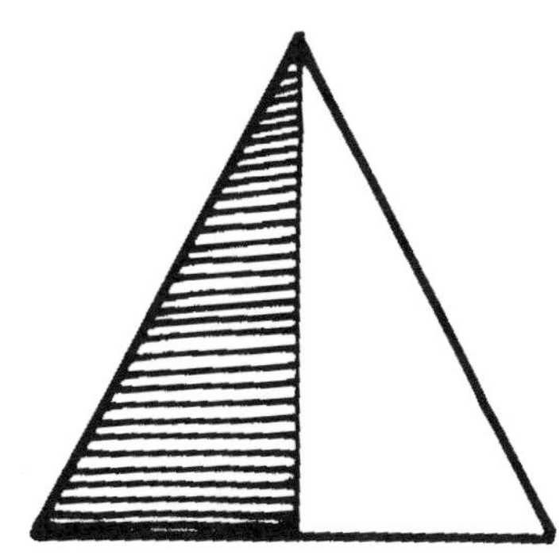

____

5. These are Antonio's crayons.

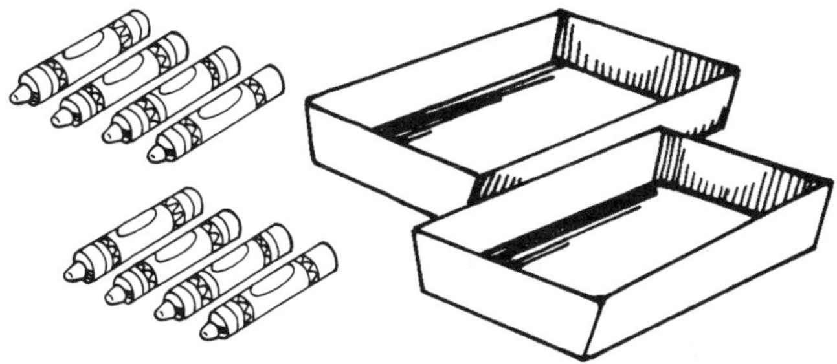

How many should he put in each box so that the boxes are equal?

A. 5 B. 8 C. 4

6. What fraction of the rectangle has polka dots?

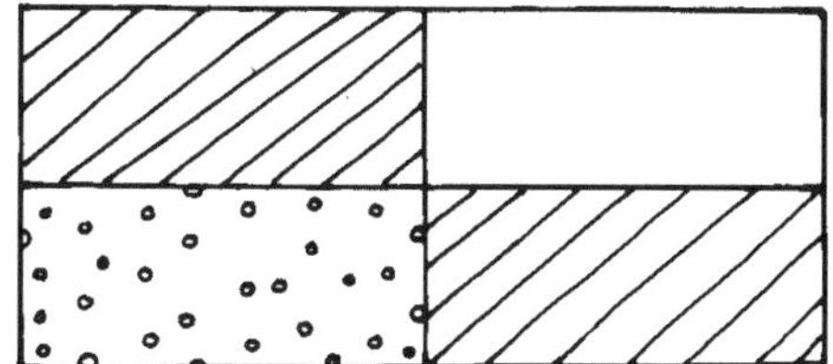

____

Longer or Shorter?

To the Teacher: Cut a piece of string 6 inches in length for each student. Ask the students to measure the classroom objects pictured below. Have them circle whether the object is **longer** or **shorter** than the string.

1. student desk

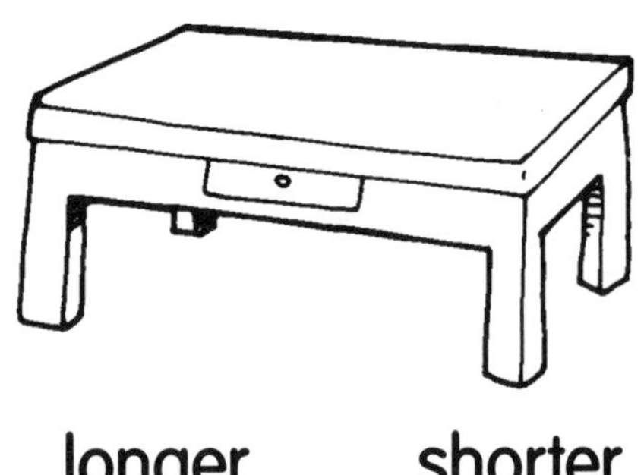

longer **shorter**

2. white board or chalkboard

Today is Monday.

The date is: __________

longer **shorter**

3. storybook

longer **shorter**

4. crayon

longer **shorter**

5. paper clip

longer **shorter**

6. piece of paper

longer **shorter**

Name ______________________________

Estimation Station

Directions: Look at this paper clip.
How many paper clips do you think it would take to measure each object?
Write your answer on the blank.

1.

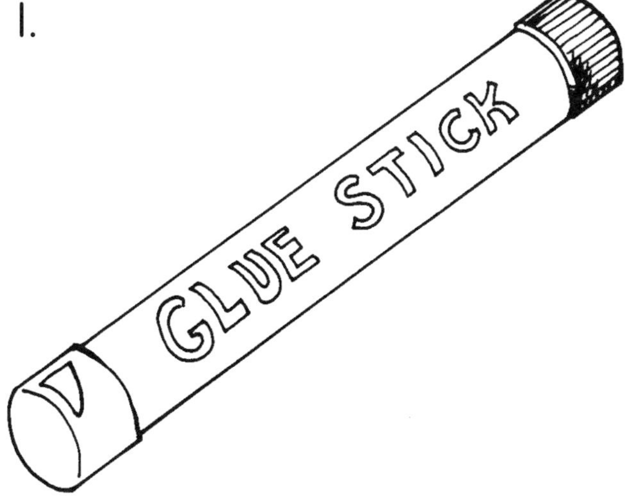

______ paper clips

2.

______ paper clips

3.

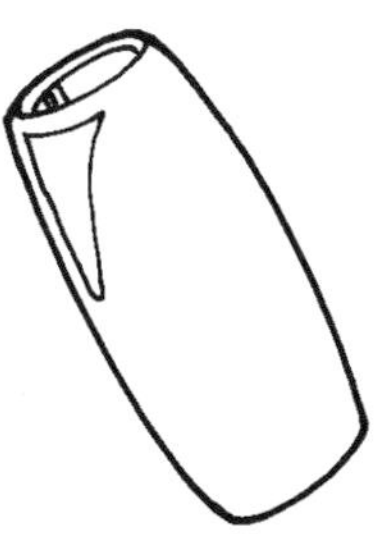

______ paper clips

4.

______ paper clips

Paper-Clip Measurement

Note to the Teacher: Give each student 8–10 standard (rubber-coated) paper clips. Encourage the students to make paper-clip chains.

Directions: Use the paper clips to measure these objects in your classroom.

1. glue bottle

_____ paper clips

4. ruler

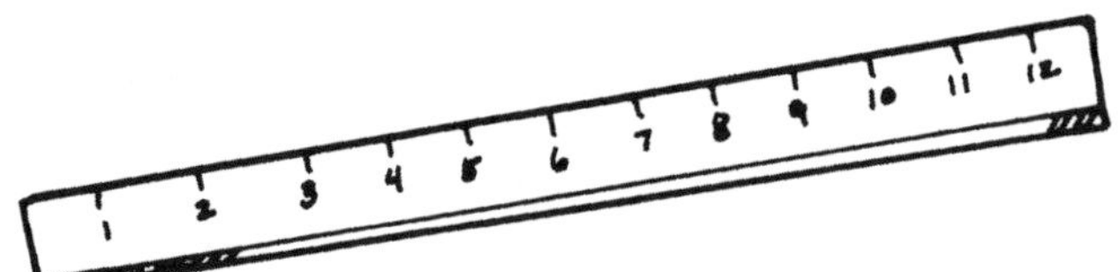

_____ paper clips

2. calendar

_____ paper clips

5. hall pass

_____ paper clips

3. abacus

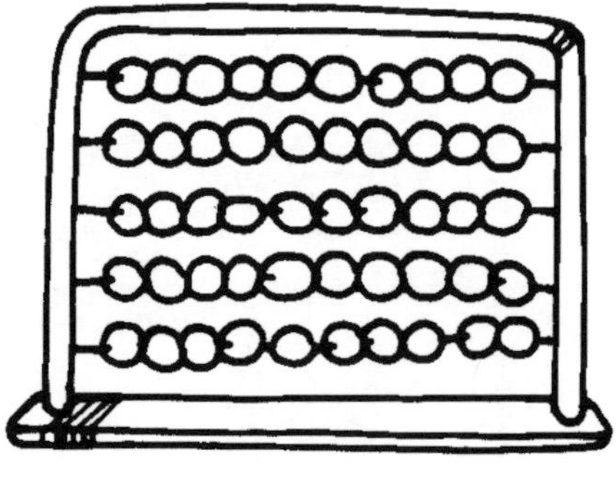

_____ paper clips

6. audio tape

_____ paper clips

Measure This: Inches

Directions: Cut out the ruler below. Measure the following pictures.

1.

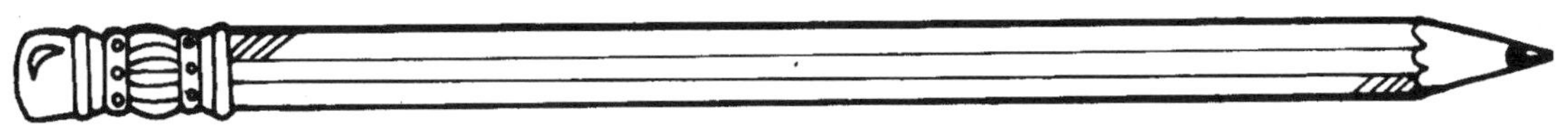

_____ inches

2.

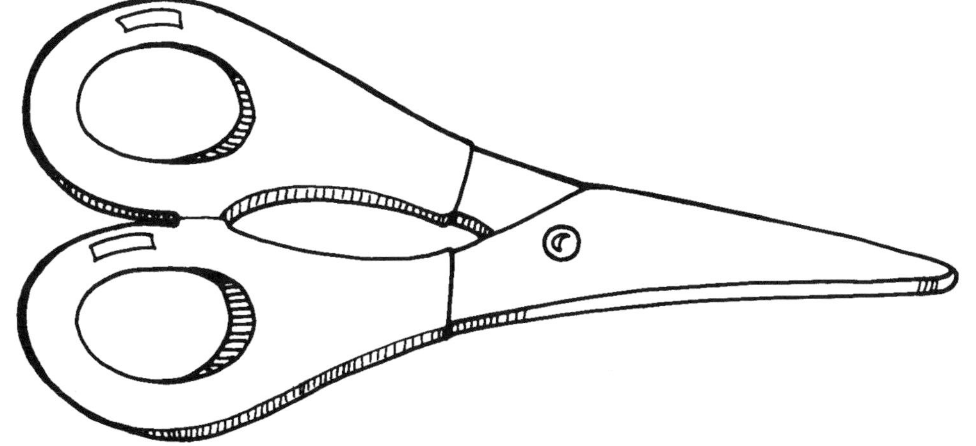

_____ inches

3.

_____ inches

0 1 2 3 4 5 6 7

Name ____

Distance: Near or Far?

Note to the Teacher: Use this page as a discussion starter. Either reproduce this page for each of your students or make an overhead transparency.

Bonus: What other things can you think of that are near or far?

Which Is Heavier? Cut and Paste

Directions: Look at each balance scale. One object is already on the balance scale. Which of the objects at the bottom of the page are **heavier** or **lighter**? Cut out and paste your answers.

1.

3.

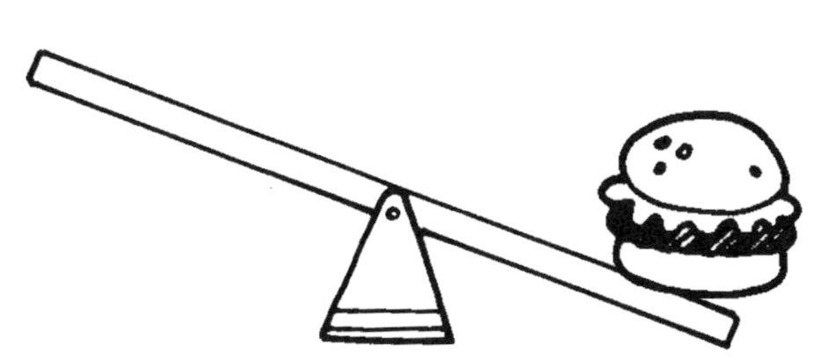

2.

4.

Name ______________________________

Pound for Pound

Explanation: When objects are placed on a scale, they are measured in pounds. For example, a house cat may weigh about 7 pounds.

Directions: Look at each object. About how many pounds do you think each object weighs? Circle your guess.

1. baby
   - **10 pounds**
   - **60 pounds**
   - **100 pounds**

2. storybook
   - **1 pound**
   - **8 pounds**
   - **10 pounds**

3. child
   - **10 pounds**
   - **30 pounds**
   - **100 pounds**

4. watermelon
   - **1 pound**
   - **5 pounds**
   - **20 pounds**

5. elephant
   - **121 pounds**
   - **1,500 pounds**
   - **250 pounds**

6. police car
   - **300 pounds**
   - **800 pounds**
   - **2,000 pounds**

Which Holds More?

Directions: Look at each set of pictures. Circle the object that holds more liquid.

1.

bathtub

swimming pool

2.

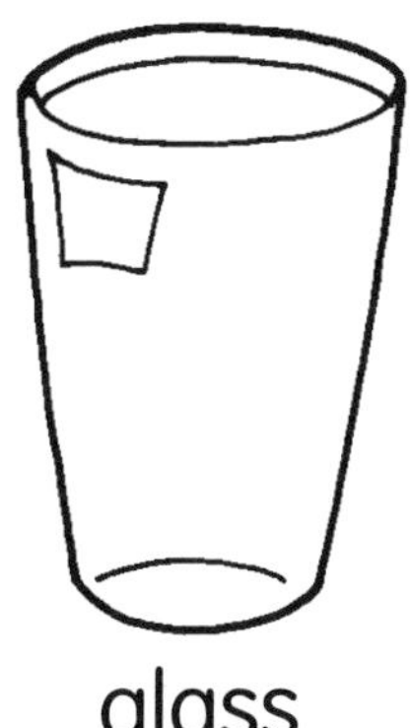

glass

mug

3.

fishbowl

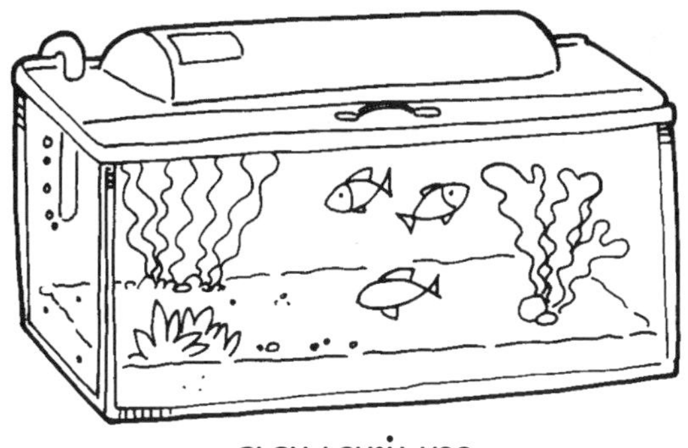

aquarium

4.

bucket

bottle

Name ______________________________

Fruit Punch: Liquid Measurement

Liquid is measured for a recipe using these containers and sizes.

Simple Classroom Fruit Punch

Ingredients:
- 2 quarts of apple juice
- 2 pints of grape juice
- 1 pint of cranberry juice
- 2 cups of ginger ale
- 3 cups of ice

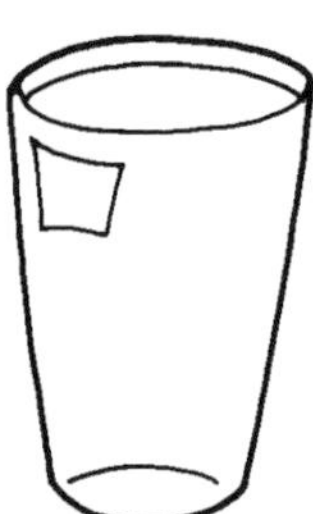

Utensils Needed:
- plastic measuring containers (1 cup, 1 pint, 1 quart)
- punch bowl
- spoon for stirring
- paper drinking cups

Directions: Mix all ingredients together in a punch bowl. Stir well. Add ice and serve. Use the recipe to answer the following questions.

1. 2 cups of ginger ale =

   ______ **pint of ginger ale**

2. 2 pints of grape juice =

   ______ **quart of grape juice**

3. How many quarts are in 1 gallon?

   ______ **quarts**

4. **Challenge: Organize the children into teams to solve the following question.** How much fruit punch is made with this recipe, not counting the ice?

   A. **1 quart** C. **1 pint**
   B. **1 gallon** D. **2 quarts**

Homework: Measure Me!

Dear Parents,

We have been studying different units of measurement (length, weight, and capacity). You may want to strengthen your child's understanding further by reading *Inch by Inch,* by Leo Lionni (Scholastic, 1960) or *Hershey's Milk Chocolate Weights and Measures,* by Jerry Pallotta (Scholastic, 2002).

Below are some fun activities to do at home to reinforce your child's understanding of different units of measurement.

Activity 1 Measure your child with either a ruler, a measuring tape, or a yardstick.
How tall is your child? ____ inches.
Have your child measure you.
How many inches tall are you? _____ inches.
Discuss the measurements with your child.

Activity 2 Weigh your child on a scale.
How much does your child weigh? ______ pounds.
Then weigh your family cat or dog.
How much does the animal weigh? ______ pounds.
Discuss the difference in weights with your child.

Activity 3 Does your child have any friends or relatives that live in another city or state? If yes, find where they live on a map. Then show your child where you live on the map. Is the friend or relative near or far from where you live? Have your child write a letter to this relative or friend.

Activity 4 Invite your child to help you in the kitchen. Your child can measure liquids, hand you utensils and ingredients, or fill up pots and pans with cool water. Talk about recipes and how ingredients are measured. Let your child take an active part in the cooking process. Don't be afraid to make a mess!

Problem Solving

Directions: Solve the following problems.

1. Find and look at a ruler.

   A. How many inches are on the ruler?

   ________ **inches**

   B. How many rulers tall are you?

   ________ **rulers**

2. A. Which container holds more?

A. B.

B. Why? **It is bigger.**
It is smaller.
It has a straw in it.

3. **Challenge**: What equals 1 quart?

   A. **2 pints**

   B. **4 cups**

   C. **neither**

   D. **both**

4. Circle which tool you would use to weigh a dog.

5. Look at this piece of paper.
   About how many crayons long do you think it is?

   A. ______ crayons

   B. Take out some crayons and measure the paper.
   How many crayons long is it?

   ________ **crayons**

6.

Color the **longest** rectangle **blue**.
Color the **shortest** rectangle **red**.
Color the other 2 rectangles **green**.
Are the green rectangles the same length?

yes or **no**

Clock Face and Hands

Some clocks have a face 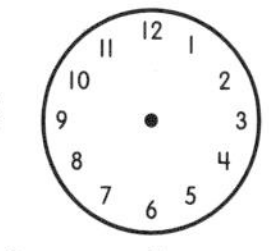 and two hands .

We use the **face** and the **hands** to tell what time it is.
The **big hand** tells the **minutes** and the **little hand** tells the **hours**.

Example:

When the **big hand** is pointing to the 12 and the **little hand** is on the 3, that tells us it is 3 o'clock.

1. Write the missing numbers on the clock.
2. Color the little (hour) hand red.
3. Color the big (minute) hand blue.
4. What time does this clock show?

________ : 00

Name ______________________________

What Time Is It?

Explanation: Explain to the children the concept of a half hour. Show them examples on a classroom clock.

Directions: Look at the clock examples. Then fill in the blanks to tell what time it is.

1. 
9:00

5. 
3:30

2. 
____:____

6. 
____:____

3. 
____:____

7. 
____:____

4. 
____:____

8. 
____:____

Name ______________________________

How Long Does It Take?

How long does it take you to do certain things? Do you spend lots of time on things you like to do? There are **60 minutes** in **one hour**. There are **24 hours** in **one day**.

Directions: Look at each picture below.
Circle about how much time it takes to do each activity.

1. ride the school bus

1 minute

15 minutes

2 hours

4. watch 2 or 3 favorite TV shows

3 minutes

20 minutes

2 hours

2. listen to a math lesson

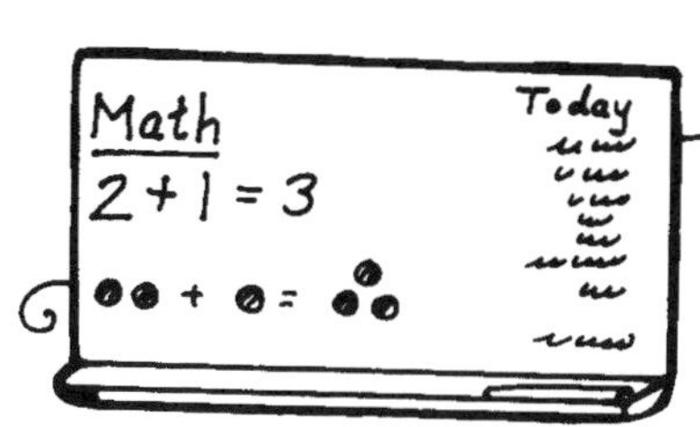

10 minutes

55 minutes

6 hours

5. do homework

1 hour

5 hours

10 hours

3. do 20 jumping jacks

2 minutes

10 minutes

30 minutes

6. read a story before bed

3 minutes 35 minutes 3 hours

Name ______________________________

Matching Time: Cut and Paste

There are two kinds of clocks.

This is a clock you may see in your kitchen or classroom.

Both clocks tell the same time.

This is a clock you may see in your bedroom. It has an alarm.

Directions: Cut out the clocks at the bottom of the page.
Paste each clock next to the clock that tells the same time.

1.

4.  5:00

2. 4:00

5.

3. 6:30

6.

1:00

3:00

2:30

Name ___________________________________

Morning, Noon, Day, and Night

When we wake up, it is **morning**. The time may be 6:30 a.m.
When we go to bed, it is **night**. The time may be 8:00 p.m.
Time changes from a.m. to p.m. at noon (12:00 p.m.).

Directions: Look at the pictures. Are these events happening during the **day** or **night**? Is it **a.m.** or **p.m.**? Circle your answers.

1. eating breakfast

day a.m.

night p.m.

2. picnic lunch

day a.m.

night p.m.

3. playing baseball after school

day a.m.

night p.m.

4. going to sleep

day a.m.

night p.m.

Name ______________________________

Time and Events

Directions: Think about the things you do each day.
Draw a line from the event to the time it usually takes place.

1. arrive at school

4:00 p.m.

2. eat lunch

6:30

6:30 a.m.

3. wake up and brush your teeth

11:30 a.m.

4. fly a kite outside

8:00 p.m.

5. read a bedtime story

9:00 a.m.

Name ______________________________

Days and Months

Directions: Answer the following questions by filling in the blanks.

There are 7 days in a week:

Sunday Monday Tuesday Wednesday Thursday Friday Saturday

1. How many days are in each week? ______________________________

2. Which 2 days begin with the letter "T"? ______________________ and ______________________

3. What day is the end of the school week? ______________________

4. What is your favorite day of the week?______________________

There are 12 months in a year:

January February March April May June July August, September October November December

5. A. How many months start with the letter "J"? ______________________

   B. What are those months? ______________________

6. In which month is Thanksgiving? ______________________

7. School starts in which month? ______________________

8. A. What is your favorite month of the year? ______________________

   B. Why? ______________________

Name ______________________________

Color the Calendar

Directions: Use the calendar to answer the following questions.

March

Sunday	Monday	Tuesday	Wednesday	Thursday	Friday	Saturday
		1	2	3	4	5
6	7	8	9	10	11	12
13	14	15	16	17 St. Patrick's Day	18	19
20	21	22	23	24	25	26
27	28	29	30	31		

1. The first day of every week is ______________________________.
2. What month does this calendar show? ____________________.
3. On what day of the week is St. Patrick's Day? ________________.
4. Draw a ☺ on the last day of the month.
5. Color all of the Saturdays yellow.
6. Put a X on the first day of the month.
7. Color the second Monday green.
8. Color the fourth Wednesday blue.

Challenge: Place a ✓ on all the days that you do not go to school this month.

Name ______________________________

Simply Seasons!

To the teacher: Discuss the seasons with the students before giving them this activity page.

Directions: Look at the pictures. Write the matching name of the season.

Word Bank:	fall	winter	spring	summer

1. ______________________________

2. ______________________________

3. ______________________________

4. ______________________________

Name ________________________________

Counting with Pennies

A **penny** is worth one cent.  I penny = I¢

Directions: Count the number of pennies in each box. Write the answer on the blank.

1.

_______ ¢

2.

_______ ¢

3.

_______ ¢

4.

_______ ¢

Name ______________________________

Nickels in a Piggy Bank

A **nickel** is worth five cents.  **1 nickel = 5¢**

Directions: Count the number of nickels in the piggy bank.
Hint: When counting the value of nickels, count by 5s. For example, 5 nickels = 25¢

1. Number of nickels in the piggy bank: ______ = ________¢

2. Number of nickels on the page: ______ = _______¢

Name ______________________________

A Jar Full of Dimes: Cut and Paste

A **dime** is worth ten cents.  **1 dime = 10¢**

Directions: Look at the cents listed by each jar. Cut and paste the correct number of dimes in the jars. **Hint:** When counting the value of dimes, count by 10s.

1. 70¢

2. 40¢

3. 

* Challenge 85¢

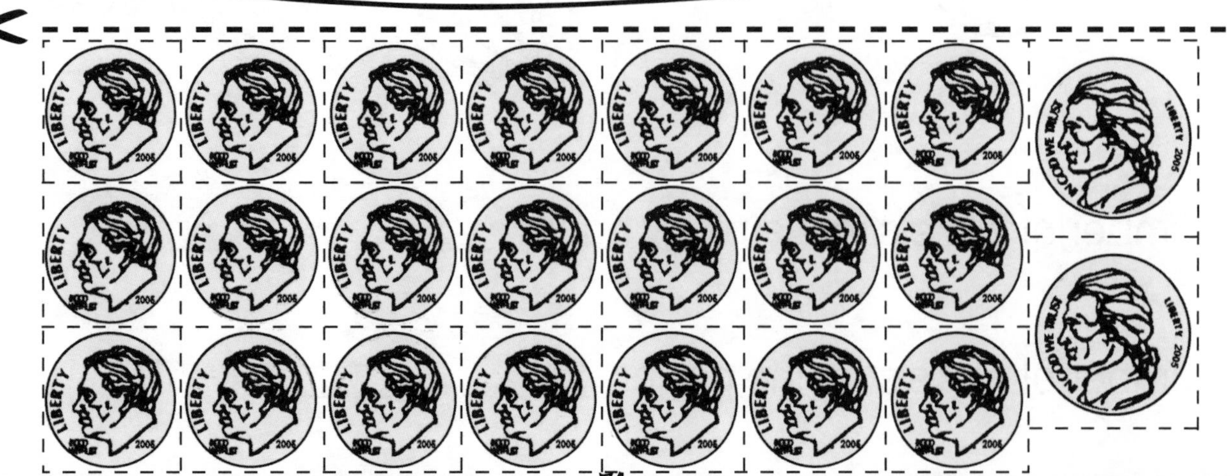

What's in Washington's Head?

A **quarter** is worth twenty-five cents. I quarter = 25¢

For example: 4 quarters = $1.00 because 25¢ + 25¢ + 25¢ + 25¢ = 100¢

Directions: Draw a circle around each set of 4 quarters inside George Washington's head. Count the sets. How many dollars do you count?

I quarter = 25¢
2 quarters = 50¢
3 quarters = 75¢
4 quarters = $1.00

I. How many sets of 4 quarters are there?

____

2. How many quarters are in George Washington's head?

____

3. How many dollars are there?

____

Buying with Dollars and Cents

When buying items, sometimes we pay with dollar bills and coins.

A **dollar bill** is worth one dollar. **1 dollar = $1.00**

Directions: Circle the money you would use to buy each item.

1. 15¢

2. 34¢

3. $1.05

4. 67¢

Name ______________________________

Homework: Coupons Galore

Parents,

We have been studying different units of time and money. You may want to strengthen your child's understanding of these concepts by reading *My First Book of Time,* by Claire Llewellyn (Dorling Kindersley, 1992) or *Alexander, Who Used to Be Rich Last Sunday,* by Judith Viorst (Atheneum, 1978).

Activity 1 Look in a Sunday newspaper for a grocery store flyer. Have your child choose items to "buy." Write down the prices of these items. Then look for coupons for these items. Subtract the amount of the coupon from the grocery-store price.

Activity 2 Have your child cut out eight coupons for items you might like to buy. Add the savings two coupons at a time. Now have fun shopping with your child while you save money!

Name ______________________________

Problem Solving

Directions: Solve the following problems.

1. How much money is this?

_________ ¢

2. Do these clocks show the same time?

yes   no

3. In what season is the Fourth of July?

spring   summer

winter   fall

4. Which will take the longest time?

A. sleeping all night

B. eating lunch

C. reading a story

5.

Sun	Mon	Tues	Wed	Thur	Fri	Sat
1	2	3	4	5	6	7
8	9	10	11	12	13	14 ♡
15	16	17	18	19	20	21
22	23	24	25	26	27	28

♡ = Valentine's Day

A. What month is this?

January   February   March

B. How do you know? _______________

____

6. Circle the coins needed to buy this toy.

All, Some, or None

Directions: Look at the trees. Are **all** of the apples on the tree, are **some** of the apples on the tree, or are **none** of the apples on the tree? Circle the correct answer.

1.

A. On the tree: **all** **some** **none**

B. On the ground: **all** **some** **none**

2.

A. On the tree: **all** **some** **none**

B. On the ground: **all** **some** **none**

3.

A. On the tree: **all** **some** **none**

B. On the ground: **all** **some** **none**

Animal Tally

A tally mark is a mark used when counting. Make one tally mark (|) for each item. After four items, make the fifth mark like this: ~~||||~~.

Directions: Count the animals. Make tally marks to show the number of each kind of animal. The fish have been counted for you.

1. fish	||||
2. birds	
3. cats	
4. mice	
5. dogs	

6. What 2 animals have the same number? ______________________.

Name ______________________

Reading a Pictograph: Cut and Paste

A **pictograph** is a graph that uses pictures to show how many.

Directions: Use the tally chart to see how many books each student can read in one week. Cut out the books from the bottom of the page. Glue them on the graph.

Student	Tally
Mandy	|||
Renee	~~||||~~	
Keith	||||
Eric	||

Student	Books
Mandy	
Renee	
Keith	
Eric	

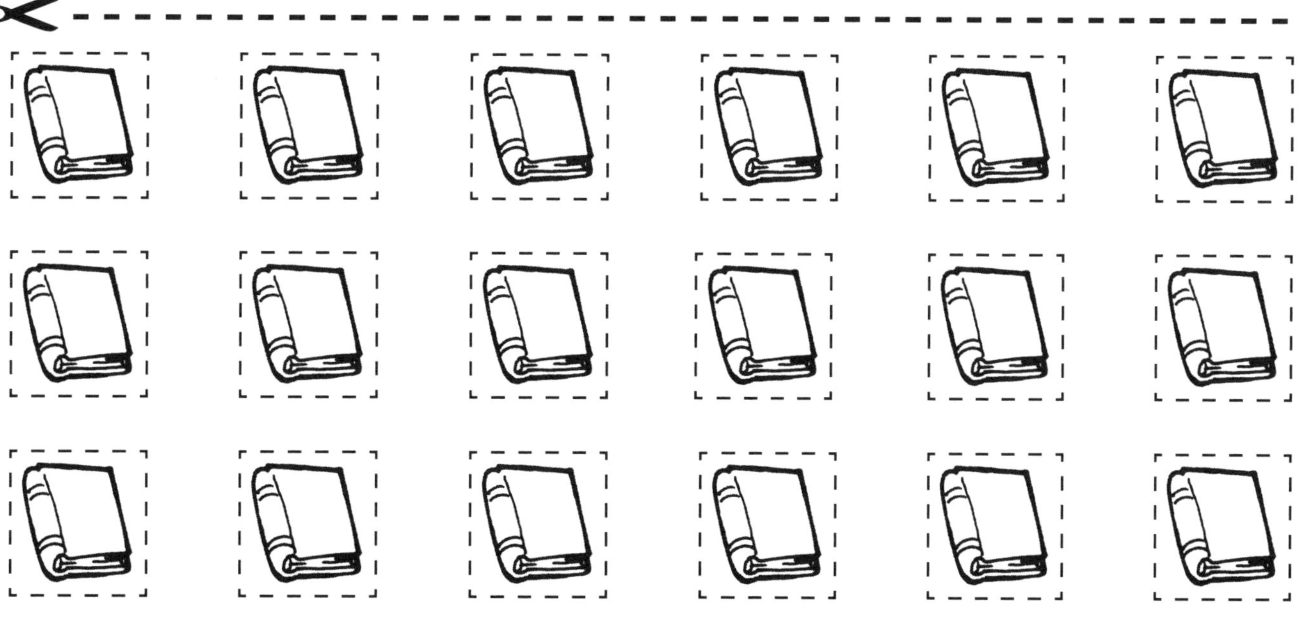

Name ____

Creating an Ice Cream-Bar Graph

Directions: It is summertime at Rooster's Ice Cream Shop! Rooster sells five different kinds of ice cream bars. Look at the graph and then answer the questions.

Butter pecan					
Cherry					
Strawberry					
Vanilla					
Chocolate					

1. Which kind of ice cream bar did children buy the most? ____________________

2. Which kinds of ice cream bars sold equally? ____________________

3. Which kind of ice cream bar sold the least? ____________________

4. Which kind of ice cream bar is your favorite? ____________________

Homework: Graphing at Home

Dear Parents,

We have been studying different types of charts and graphs. You may want to reinforce your child's understanding of these concepts by reading *The Very Busy Spider,* by Eric Carle, (Philomel, 1984) or *Caps for Sale,* by Esphyr Slobodkina, (Harper Collins, 1947).

Activity 1 Use the illustration below to make a tally chart of male and female relatives in your family. Be sure to include all sisters, brothers, cousins, aunts, uncles, and grandparents.

Activity 2 Using the illustration below make either a pictograph or bar graph to represent the members of your family.

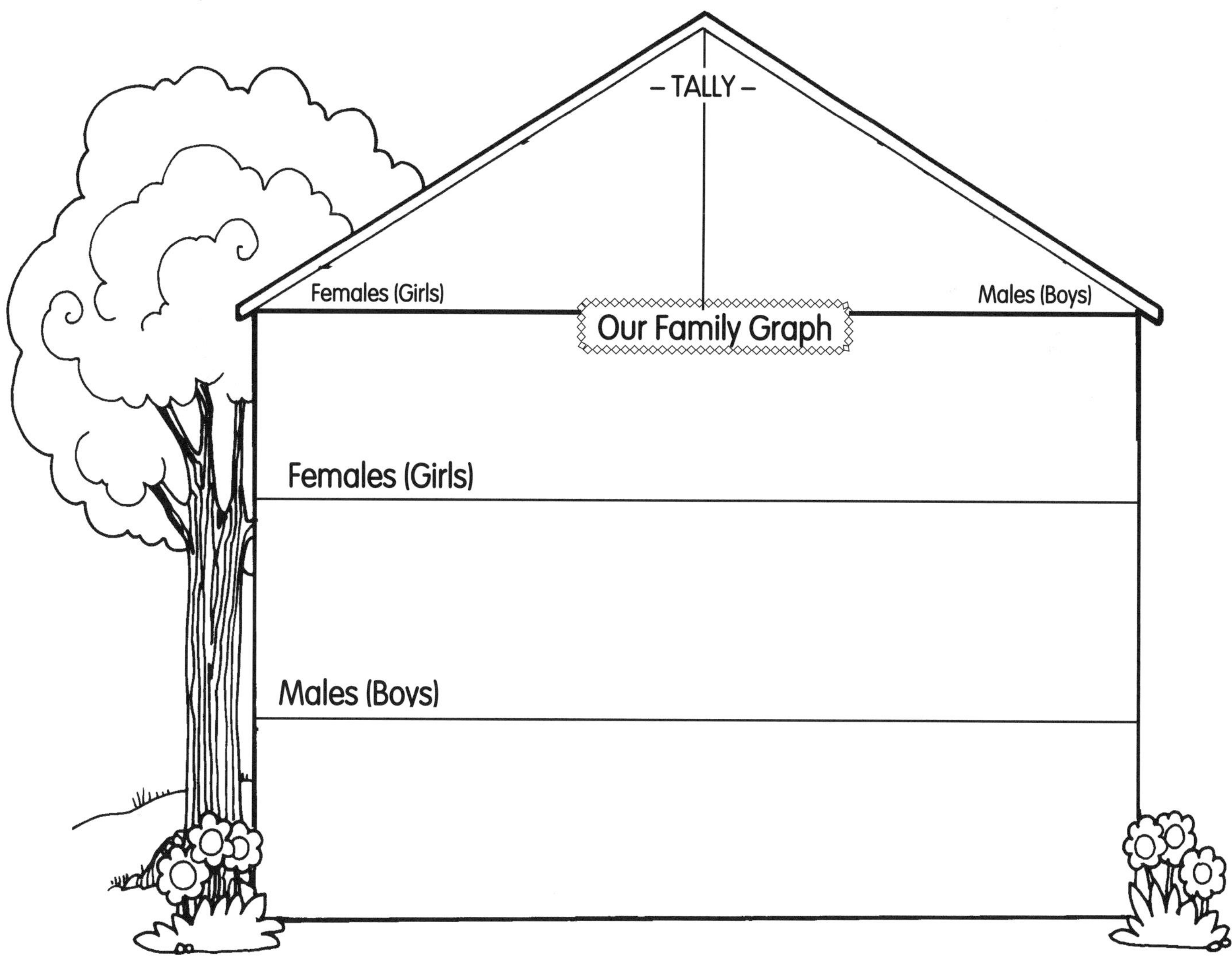

Name ______________________________

Problem Solving

Directions: Solve the following problems.
Use the clues to fill in the tally chart, pictograph, and bar graph.

Mark has 3 cookies.
Sasha has 3 cookies plus 1 cookie (3 + 1).
Katie has 4 cookies plus 2 cookies (4 + 2).
Tim has 3 cookies minus 1 cookie (3 – 1).

1. Tally Chart

Mark	
Sasha	
Katie	
Tim	

2. **Pictograph Cookies**

Mark	
Sasha	
Katie	
Tim	

(cookie) = 1 cookie

3. **Bar Graph**

Mark						
Sasha						
Katie						
Tim						
	1	2	3	4	5	6

Posttest: Number and Operations

Directions: Solve the following problems.

1. Write the numbers that come before and after each number.

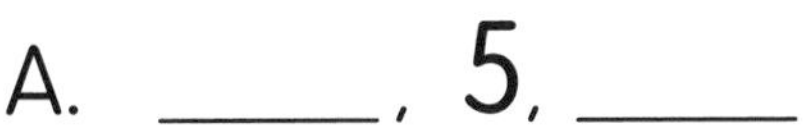

A. ____, 5, ____

B. ____, 11, ____

C. ____, 34, ____

2. Write the number words.

A. 4 ____________________

B. 7 ____________________

3. Which tree has fewer apples?

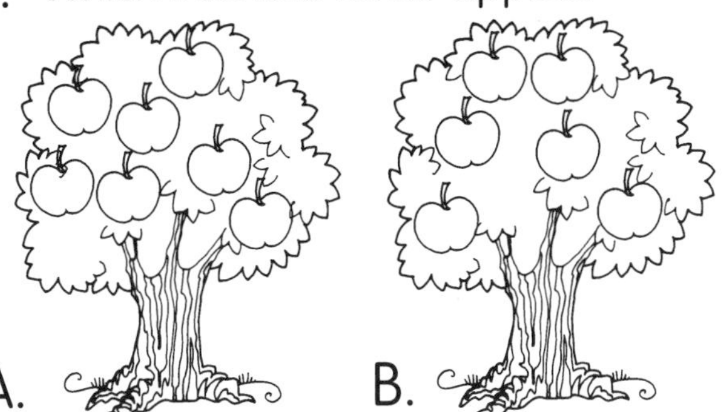

4. What number is this? __________

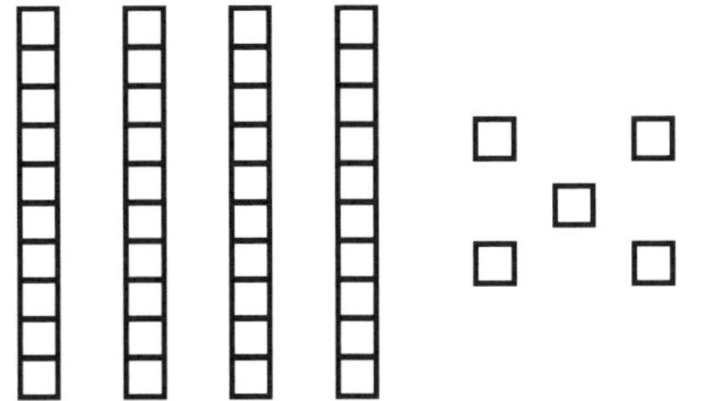

5. Which bug came in first? Circle it.

6. How many boxes of crayons do I have? Write the addition sentence.

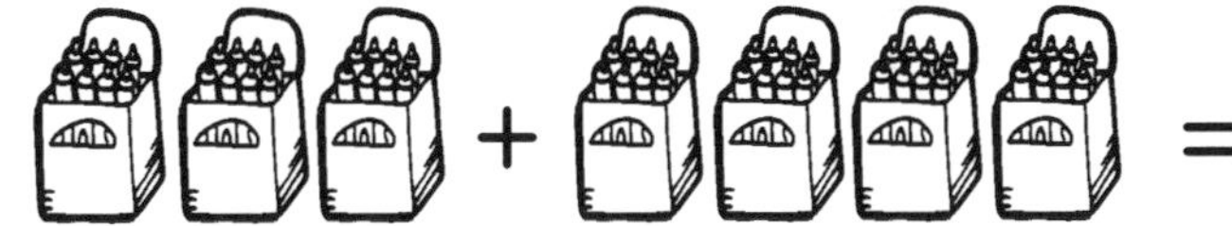

____ + ____ = ____

7. Sam had 5 chairs at his table. Jill took 2. How many chairs did Sam have left? Write the subtraction sentence.

____ − ____ = ____

8. Skip count by 2. Fill in the blanks.

4, ____, ____, 10, 12, ____,

16, ____, 20

Posttest: Beginning Algebraic Thinking

Directions: Solve the following problems.

1. Complete the AB pattern.

2. How are these objects sorted?

A. By size

B. By shape

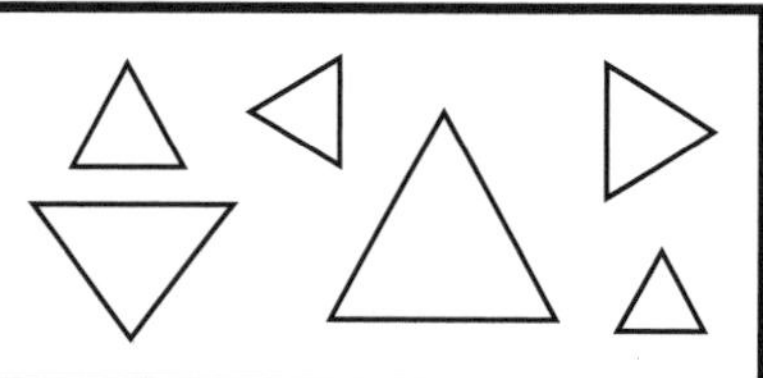

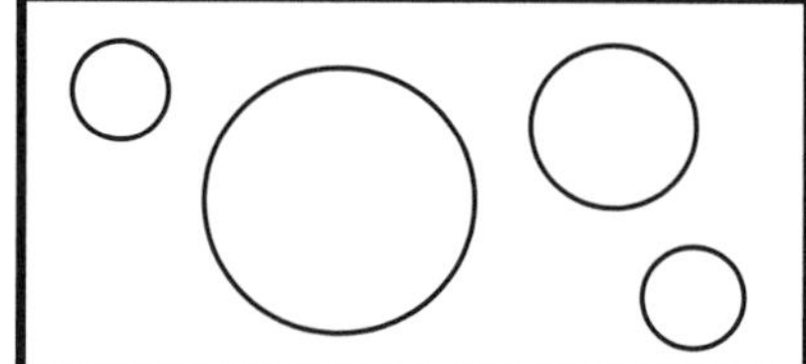

3. Which number fills in all of the blanks?

0, 1, ________, 0, ________, 1

________, 2, 1, 2, ________, 2

4. Each shape represents a number. Fill in all of the blanks?

3 + 1 = △ A. △ = ______

△ + ☐ = 7 B. ☐ = ______

5. Complete the pattern below.

cat, rat, ______, cat, ______, sat, ______, rat, sat, cat, ______

Posttest: Geometry and Fractions

Directions: Solve the following problems.

1. Which shape is most like a circle? 

oval triangle square

2. Is it a shape we have learned?

A.  yes no

B. 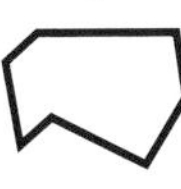 yes no

C.  yes no

3. Juan has 3 friends to share his cake. How much cake will each friend receive?

A. $\frac{1}{2}$

B. $\frac{1}{3}$

C. $\frac{1}{4}$

4. The teddy bear is **(above, below)** the box.

5. Color each shape that shows symmetry.

6. What fraction is shaded?

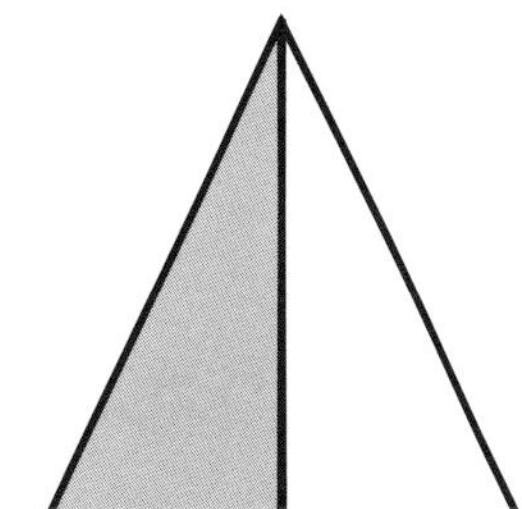

A. 1

B. $\frac{1}{2}$

C. $\frac{1}{4}$

7. Is the rectangle to the right or left of the star?

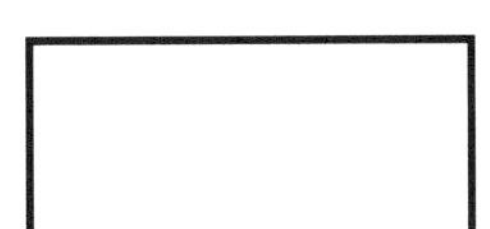

A. **left** B. **right**

8. Is the shaded area in this rectangle equal to one-third?

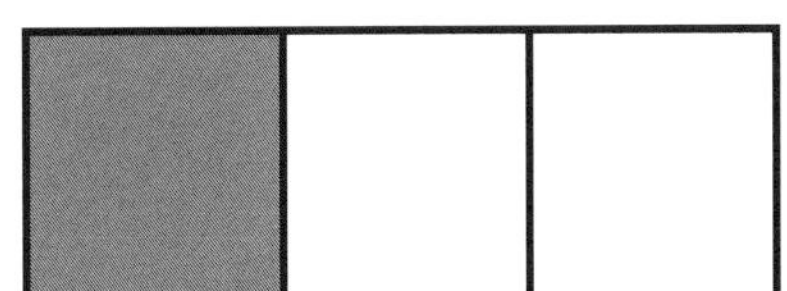

A. **yes** B. **no**

Posttest: Measurement

Directions: Solve the following problems.

1. Circle the tool used to measure inches.

2. **Estimate.** How long will your paper clip chain be to equal the length of this paper?

5 paper clips 10 paper clips

3. Are the clouds in the sky near to us or far from us?

near to far from

4. Which is heavier?

bread toast

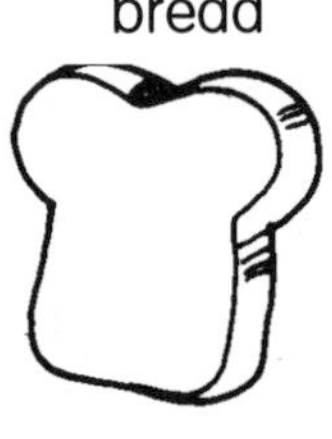

bread toast neither

5. Which holds the most water?

fishbowl cup aquarium

6. If 4 cups = 2 pints, how many pints equal 2 cups?

____

7. Is your pencil longer or shorter than this test paper?

longer shorter

8. About how much does a newborn baby weigh?

1 pound

7 pounds

18 pounds

Posttest: Time and Money

Directions: Solve the following problems.

1. When the big hand is on the 6, how many minutes do we put in the blank?

3 : ______

00

30

06

5. Which coin equals 5¢? Circle that coin.

2. About how long does a bath take?

2 minutes

20 minutes

2 hours

6. Is it true or false?

George Washington's head is on the quarter and the dollar bill.

true false

3. How much money is shown?

6 ¢

38 ¢

43 ¢

7. Do these 2 clocks show the same time?

yes no

4. Is it true or false?

There are 7 months in 1 year and 12 days in 1 week.

true false

8. 2 dimes are worth (**less than** or **more than**) 2 quarters.

less than more than

Math Web Sites

Games

http://www.coolmath-games.com

Feature Games: Arithmetic-24 . . . similar to the 24 Game sold in retail stores. IQ game. . . similar to the wood triangles with pegs that one plays at a Cracker Barrel restaurant.

http://www.funbrain.com

You can choose the grade level (K-12). Feature Game: Math baseball . . . add, subtract, multiply, or divide or do all four; three levels of play; three strikes and you're out!

http://www.aplusmath.com

Feature Games: Flash cards and concentration . . . can play either of these using one of four operations.

Teacher Resource Web Sites

http://e-math.ams.org

American Mathematical Society-eMath. The on-line home of the American Mathematical Society. This site offers information about the society, links to useful math-related sites on the Web, and some organization information.

http://archives.math.utk.edu

Math Archives—Topics in Mathematics. Here is THE math resource site on the Web. It has hundreds of links (fully searchable) in forty different categories ranging from algebra to partial differential equations.

Math Web Sites

http://www.nettrekker.com

NetTrekker—A Search Engine for Students and Teachers. This is a powerful search engine for both teachers and students. Elementary, middle, and high school math topics are included. A nominal fee is required.

http://www.aaamath.com

AAA Math . . . over 200 pages of math lessons (K-8) which feature interactive practice, challenge games, and an explanation of the topic.

http://school.discovery.com/lessonplans/math.html

Discovery Channel School: Math Lesson Plans . . . curriculum tie-ins with the programs, vocabulary, and great activities to support the metric system, length, probability, numbers in nature, and much more.

http://mathforum.org/dr.math/dr-math.html

Ask Dr. Math . . . an archive of math questions, searchable and arranged by grade level; you can also submit your own questions.

http://www.edu4kids.com/math/

Flashcards for Kids . . . an interactive, on-line, elementary math problem solver.

http://www.eduplace.com/math/index.html

Houghton Mifflin Education Place: Mathematics Center . . . links to activities, projects, and brainteasers in math.

Answer Key

Page 5
1. one; **2.** two; **3.** three; **4.** four; **5.** five

Page 6
6. six; **7.** seven; **8.** eight; **9.** nine; **10.** ten

Page 7
3 = paints; 7 = pencils; 2 = books;
6 = scissors; 4 = rulers; 5 = lunch boxes;
1 = box of crayons

Page 8
1. nine, two, five; **2.** three, eight, six;
3. four, seven, one

Page 9
1. the last two cakes
2. the middle cake
3. the first cake

Page 10
1, 4, 6, 7, 9, 12, 14, 16

Page 11
1. 23; **2.** 14; **3.** 7, 10

Page 14
1. 23; **2.** 15; **3.** 40

Page 15
1. second; **2.** fourth; **3.** first; **4.** third; **5.** fifth

Page 16
1. 7; **2.** 10; **3.** 4; **4.** 5; **5.** 10

Page 17
1. 3; **2.** 5; **3.** 7; **4.** 5; **5.** 9

Page 18
1. 8 – 5 = 3; **2.** 6 – 2 = 4; **3.** 7 – 1 = 6

Page 19
1. 4; **2.** 5; **3.** 2; **4.** 6; **5.** 2

Page 21
1. 7; **2.** 12, 15, 16, 18, 21;
3. 7; **4.** *Answers will vary.*
5. 3; **6.** mittens with three dots

Page 22
1. A = lollipop, A = lollipop; B = candy
2. B =cloud, A = sun, C = rainbow
3. B = spoon, A = fork, B = spoon
4. B = girl, B = girl, B = girl
5. A = bat, B = cap, C = baseball

Page 23

1. 

2. 

3. 

4. 

5. 

6. 

Page 24 *(Answers may vary.)*

1. 

2. 

3. 

Page 25
1. 4; **2.** 5;
3. 8; **4.** 6;
5. 3; **6.** 0

Answer Key

Page 26
1. 4; **2.** 5; **3.** 4;
4. 1; **5.** 5; **6.** 2;
7. 1; **8.** 9

Page 27
1. e; **2.** d; **3.** b; **4.** c; **5.** a

Page 28
1. d; **2.** a; **3.** b; **4.** c

Page 29 *(Answers may vary.)*
1. books, audiotapes, computer
2. pencil, paper, picture
3. teddy bear counters, ruler, clock
4. crayons, paints, scissors

Page 30
Answers will vary.

Page 31

2. A. yes; B. no; C. yes
3. A. 4, B. 3
4. seed;
5. 37, 40, 41
6. small = triangle, circle, heart;
large = rectangle, circle, square

Page 32
1. clock, baseball;
2. *Answers will vary.*
3. olives, Easter eggs;
4. *Answers will vary.*

Page 33
1. book, stamp, gift
2. *Answers will vary.*
3. pie, hanger, pizza

Page 34
1–3. *Answers will vary.*

Page 35
1. no; **2.** yes; **3.** yes;
4. no; **5.** yes; **6.** yes;
7. no; **8.** no;
9. yes; **10.** yes

Page 36
2. smaller than
3. larger than
4. smaller than
5. larger than

Pages 37-38 *Answers will vary.*

Page 39
2. no; **3.** yes;
4. yes; **5.** no; **6.** yes;
7. yes; **8.** no

Page 40
2. quarter; **3.** picture; **4.** pizza; **5.** television

Page 41
2. B4; **3.** flute; **4.** drum

Page 42
1. above; **2.** under;
3. left; **4.** right;
5. near

Page 43
Answers will vary.

Page 44
1. rectangle;
2. circle = red, star = yellow, oval = blue
3. *Answers will vary.*
4. *Answers will vary.*
5. 1;
6. triangle

Answer key

Page 45
Each box will have the following:
1. 1 or 3 keys; **2.** 2 keys; **3.** 1 or 3 keys

Page 46
1. half; **2.** whole;
3. half; **4.** whole;
5. whole; **6.** half

Page 47
1. no; **2.** no; **3.** yes; **4.** yes

Page 48
1. no; **2.** yes; **3.** yes; **4.** yes

Page 49
1. 1/2; **2.** 1/2; **3.** 1/3
4. 1/4; **5.** 1; **6.** 1/4

Page 51
1. C; **2.** 1/2 blue, 1/4 yellow;
3. B; **4.** 1/2;
5. C; **6.** 1/4

Page 52
1. longer; **2.** longer;
3. longer; **4.** shorter;
5. shorter; **6.** longer

Page 53
Answers will vary.

Page 54
Answers will vary.

Page 55
1. 6 inches
2. 5 inches
3. 2 inches

Page 56
1. near; **2.** far; **3.** far; **4.** near

Page 57 *(Suggested Answers)*
1. pumpkin; **2.** bread or pie; **3.** key or egg
4. drum

Page 58
1. 10 pounds; **2.** 1 pound;
3. 100 pounds; **4.** 5 pounds;
5. 1,500 pounds;
6. 2,000 pounds

Page 59
1. swimming pool;
2. glass
3. aquarium
4. bucket

Page 60
1. 1 pint; **2.** 1 quart;
3. 4 quarts; **4.** B

Page 61
Answers will vary.

Page 62
1. A. 12; B. *Answers will vary.*
2. A. A, B. It is bigger.
3. D
4. scale
5. *Answers will vary.*
6. green, blue, green, red, yes

Page 63
1. 2, 7, 10; **2.** little hand = red;
3. big hand = blue; **4.** 8:00

Page 64
2. 1:00; **3.** 10:00; **4.** 1:30; **6.** 4:00; **7.** 8:30; **8.** 11:30

Answer Key

Page 65 *Answers may vary.*
1. 15 minutes; **2.** 55 minutes; **3.** 2 minutes;
4. 2 hours; **5.** 1 hour; **6.** 35 minutes

Page 66
1. 1:00; **2.** 4:00; **3.** 6:30;
4. 5:00; **5.** 2:30; **6.** 3:00

Page 67
1. day, a.m.; **2.** day, p.m.; **3.** day, p.m.;
4. night, p.m.

Page 68
1. 9:00 a.m.; **2.** 11:30 a.m.; **3.** 6:30 a.m.;
4. 4:00 p.m.; **5.** 8:00 p.m.

Page 69
1. 7; **2.** Tuesday, Thursday;
3. Friday; **4.** *Answers will vary.*
5. A. 3, B. January, June, July;
6. November; **7.** August or September;
8. *Answers will vary.*

Page 70
1. Sunday; **2.** March;
3. Thursday; **4.** March 31st

Page 71
1. winter; **2.** summer;
3. fall; **4.** spring

Page 72
1. 5¢; **2.** 2¢; **3.** 4¢; **4.** 9¢

Page 73
1. 8 = 40¢
2. 20 = 100¢ ($1.00)

Page 74
1. 7 dimes
2. 4 dimes
3. 8 dimes, 1 nickel

Page 75
1. 3; **2.** 12; **3.** $3.00

Page 76
1. 1 dime, 1 nickel; **2.** 3 dimes, 4 pennies;
3. 1 dollar, 1 nickel;
4. 2 quarters, 1 dime, 1 nickel, 2 pennies

Page 78
1. 21¢; **2.** no; **3.** summer; **4.** A;
5. A. February, B. only 28 days or Valentine's Day;
6. 1 quarter, 2 pennies

Page 79
1. A. some; B. some; **2.** A. all; B. none;
3. A. none, B. all

Page 80
2. birds–5; **3.** cats–2; **4.** mice–4; **5.** dogs–6;
6. fish and mice

Page 81
Mandy–3 books; Renee–6 books; Keith–4 books;
Eric–2 books

Page 82
1. chocolate; **2.** vanilla and butter pecan;
3. cherry; **4.** *Answers will vary.*

Page 83
Answers will vary.

Page 84
1. Tally Chart: Mark, 3; Sasha, 4; Katie, 6; Tim, 2
2. Pictograph: Mark, 3; Sasha, 4; Katie, 6; Tim, 2
3. Bar Graph: Mark, 3; Sasha, 4; Katie, 6; Tim, 2

Page 85
1. A. 4, 6, B. 10, 12, C. 33, 35;
2. A. four, B. seven;
3. B; **4.** 45; **5.** ;
6. 3 + 4 = 7; **7.** 5 – 2 = 3; **8.** 6, 8, 14, 18

Answer Key

Page 86
1. circle, triangle, circle; **2.** B; **3.** 1; **4.** A. 4, B. 3;
5. sat, rat, cat, rat

Page 87
1. oval; **2.** A. yes, B. no, C. yes;
3. C; **4.** above; **5.** heart, square;
6. B; **7.** A; **8.** A

Page 88
1. ruler; **2.** 10 paper clips; **3.** far from; **4.** neither;
5. aquarium; **6.** 1 pint; **7.** shorter; **8.** 7 pounds

Page 89
1. 3:30; **2.** 20 minutes; **3.** 38¢; **4.**false;
5. nickel; **6.** true; **7.** no; **8.** less than